Ed. 1728

THE MAGIC FLUTE

(DIE ZAUBERFLÖTE)

An Opera in Two Acts

Music by

W. A. MOZART

The Original Text by
EMANUEL SCHIKANEDER
and
CARL LUDWIG GIESECKE

With an English Version by
RUTH and THOMAS MARTIN
(As revised for the Metropolitan Opera, New York, 1951.)

ISBN 0-7935-0766-9

G. SCHIRMER, Inc.

DISTRIBUTED BY

HAL•LEONARD®
CORPORATION

7777 W. BLUEMOUND RD. P.O. BOX 13819 MILWAUKEE, WI 53213

NOTE

PREFACE

On the playbill of its first performance, September 30, 1791, *The Magic Flute* was indicated as being by Emanuel Schikaneder; and, in a footnote, the music was credited to Wolfgang Amadeus Mozart, the conductor of the orchestra that evening. Actually, Schikaneder had been only partly responsible for the book of the opera: as manager of the theater and as one of the principal comedians, he had elaborated the part of Papageno, which he played (in fact, the original librettos were illustrated with two copper-engravings of Schikaneder in his Papageno costume.) A member of the chorus, Carl Ludwig Giesecke, was probably more responsible than Schikaneder for the book as a whole. In making up the story, he had used various romantic motifs then popular, particularly as found in Wieland's Oriental fairy-tale collection *Dschinnistan*, and had mingled with them various elements taken from Freemasonry and from the social and political affairs of the day.

The first act is concerned with the quest of Prince Tamino and the bird-catcher Papageno for Pamina, the lovely daughter of the Queen of the Night. Pamina has been stolen by Sarastro, high Priest of Isis and Osiris. Tamino finally discovers that Sarastro has abducted her for her own good, to keep her away from the evil influence of her mother. By the aid of a magic flute and a set of magic bells, Tamino, Pamina, and Papageno are momentarily brought together.

The second act is concerned with the initiation of Tamino and Papageno into the mysteries of Isis and Osiris, Tamino being actuated by a love of wisdom, Papageno merely by a desire for a wife—for his long-wished-for Papagena. The Priests tell the two young men that during their probation they must not talk to any women. Pamina misunderstands Tamino's silence, and is broken-hearted. Papageno repeatedly talks when he is not supposed to, and almost loses his Papagena. But the magic flute and bells solve all difficulties, and the two happy pairs are at last united.

DRAMATIS PERSONAE

TAMINO, *an Egyptian prince*
THREE LADIES, *attendants of the Queen of the Night*
PAPAGENO, *a bird-catcher*
THE QUEEN OF THE NIGHT
THREE SLAVES
MONOSTATOS, *a Moor, servant of Sarastro*
PAMINA, *daughter of the Queen of the Night*
THREE SPIRITS
THREE PRIESTS *of the temple*
SARASTRO, *High Priest of Isis and Osiris*
OLD WOMAN (later PAPAGENA)
TWO MEN IN ARMOR

Priests, Slaves, People, etc.

39678

INDEX

Playbill of the First Performance of *The Magic Flute*

The Magic Flute
Die Zauberflöte

Original Libretto by
Emanuel Schikaneder and Carl Ludwig Giesecke
English Version by Ruth and Thomas Martin

Wolfgang Amadeus Mozart

Overture

*Orchestral material may be rented from the Publishers.

Adagio

Allegro

Act I

(Rough, rocky landscape)

No. 1. Introduction

Tamino *(runs in, pursued by a serpent.)*

Zu Hül-fe! zu Hül-fe! sonst bin ich ver-
O help me, pro-tect me, my pow - ers for -

lo - ren! zu Hül - fe! zu Hül - fe! sonst bin ich ver - lo - ren! der
sake me! O help me, pro-tect me, my pow - ers for - sake me! The

li - sti - gen Schlan - ge zum Op - fer er - ko - ren, barm - her - - zi - ge Göt - ter!
treach - er - ous ser - pent will soon o - ver - take me. Ah, Heav - ens, have mer - cy!

cresc.

Schon na - het sie sich, schon na - het sie
I see it draw near, I see it draw

(The serpent becomes visible.)

sich! ach! ret - tet mich, ach! ret - tet, ret - tet, schüt - zet mich! ach schüt - zet, schüt - zet,
near! O res - cue me, pro - tect me, save me, res - cue me! O save me, save me.

(Three Ladies hurry in, with silver javelins.)

1. & 2. L.

Stirb, Un - ge - heur! durch uns - re Macht!
Die, vi - cious snake, be - fore our might!

3. L.

Stirb, Un - ge - heur! durch uns - re Macht!
Die, vi - cious snake, be - fore our might!

(He sinks, unconscious, to the ground.)

Tamino

ret - - tet, _ ret - tet, ret - tet, schüt - - zet mich.
res - - cue, save me, save me, res - - cue me!

(They kill the serpent.)

1st Lady (*watching Tamino*)

Ein hol-der Jüngling sanft und schön,
What beau-ty in his gen-tle face!

2nd Lady

so schön als ich noch nie ge-sehn!
I nev-er saw such lovely grace!

3rd Lady

Ja, ja gewiß, zum
Yes, yes, indeed, for

Ma——len schön!
art to trace!

1st & 2nd L.

Würd ich mein Herz der Lie——be weihn, so
If I should yield to love's sweet voice, This

3rd Lady

Würd ich mein Herz der Lie-be weihn, so
If I should yield to love's sweet voice, This

müßt es die-ser Jüng-ling sein, so müßt es die-ser Jüng-ling
youth in-deed would be my choice, This youth in-deed would be my

müßt es die-ser Jüng-ling sein, so müßt es die-ser Jüng-ling
youth in-deed would be my choice, This youth in-deed would be my

Tam. (*erwacht, sieht furchtsam umher*): Wo bin ich? Ist's Phantasie, dass ich noch lebe, oder hat eine höhere Macht mich gerettet? (*Steht auf und sieht umher.*) Wie?—Die bösartige Schlange liegt tot zu meinen Füssen?—(*Man hört von hinten ein Waldflötchen.*)

Tam. (*regains consciousness, looks around, frightened*): Where am I? Is it fantasy that I am still alive? Or did some higher power save me?. (*Rises and looks around.*) That vicious snake dead at my feet? (*The sound of a panpipe is heard.*)

No. 2. Song

Andante

Tamino: Was hör ich? Ha, eine männliche Gestalt nähert sich dem Tal.
What do I hear? Where am I? What a strange place! I see a queer figure approaching. *(Withdraws.observing.)*

(Papageno, dressed in a suit of feathers, hurries by, carrying a large bird-cage on his back and a pan pipe in his hands.)

Papageno

1. Der_ Vo-gel-fän-ger bin ich ja, stets lu-stig hei-sa hop-sa-sa! ich
2. Der_ Vo-gel-fän-ger bin ich ja, stets lu-stig hei-sa hop-sa-sa! ich
3. Wenn al-le Mädchen wä-ren mein, so_ tausch-te ich brav Zuk-ker ein, die

1. I___ am a man of wide-spread fame, And Pa-pa-ge-no is my name. To
2. Al-though I am a hap-py man, I al-so have a fu-ture plan. I
3. Once_ all the girls were in my net I'd keep the fair-est for my pet, My

(He whistles and then removes the cage from his back.)

(He whistles and turns to leave.)

Tam. (*tritt ihm entgegen*): Heda!
Pap.: Was da?
Tam.: Sag mir, du lustger Freund, wer du bist.
Pap.: Wer ich bin? (*Für sich:*) Dumme Frage! (*laut:*) Ein Mensch, wie du.—Wenn ich dich nun fragte, wer du bist?
Tam.: So würde ich dir antworten, dass ich aus fürstlichem Geblüt bin.
Pap.: Das ist mir zu hoch.—Musst dich deutlicher erklären, wenn ich dich verstehen soll!
Tam.: Mein Vater ist Fürst, der über viele Länder und Menschen herrscht; darum nennt man mich Prinz.
Pap.: Länder?—Menschen?—Prinz?—Sag du mir zuvor: gibt's ausser diesen Bergen auch noch Länder und Menschen?
Tam.: Viele Tausende!
Pap.: Da liess' sich eine Spekulation mit meinen Vögeln machen.
Tam.: Wie nennt man eigentlich diese Gegend?. wer beherrscht sie?
Pap.: Das kann ich dir ebensowenig beantworten, als ich weiss, wie ich auf die Welt gekommen bin.
Tam. (*lacht*): Wie? Du wüsstest nicht, wo du geboren, oder wer deine Eltern waren?
Pap.: Kein Wort!—Ich weiss nur so viel, dass nicht weit von hier meine Strohhütte steht, die mich vor Regen und Kälte schützt.
Tam.: Aber wie lebst du?
Pap.: Von Essen und Trinken, wie alle Menschen.
Tam.: Wodurch erhältst du das?
Pap.: Durch Tausch.—Ich fange für die sternflammende Königin und ihre Jungfrauen verschiedene Vögel; dafür erhalt ich täglich Speise und Trank von ihr.
Tam. (*für sich*): Sternflammende Königin?—(*Laut:*) Sag mir, guter Freund, warst du schon so glücklich, diese Göttin der Nacht zu sehen?
Pap.: Sehen?—Die sternflammende Königin sehen?— Welcher Sterbliche kann sich rühmen, sie je gesehn zu haben? (*für sich:*) Wie er mich so starr anblickt! Bald fang ich an, mich vor ihm zu fürchten. (*Laut:*) Warum siehst du so verdächtig und schelmisch nach mir?
Tam.: Weil—weil ich zweifle, ob du ein Mensch bist.—
Pap.: Wie war das?
Tam.: Nach deinen Federn, die dich bedecken, halt ich dich—(*geht auf ihn zu.*)
Pap.: Doch für keinen Vogel?—Bleib zurück, sag ich, und traue mir nicht; denn ich habe Riesenkraft. (*Für sich.*) Wenn er sich nicht bald von mir schrecken lässt, so lauf ich davon.
Tam.: Riesenkraft? (*Er sieht auf die Schlange.*) Also warst du wohl gar mein Erretter, der diese giftige Schlange bekämpfte?
Pap.: Schlange! (*Sieht sich um, weicht zitternd einige Schritte zurück.*) Ist sie tot oder lebendig?
Tam.: Freund, wie hast du dieses Ungeheuer bekämpft?— Du bist ohne Waffen.
Pap. (*hat sich wieder gefasst*): Brauch keine!—Bei mir ist ein starker Druck mit der Hand mehr als Waffen.
Tam.: Du hast sie also erdrosselt?
Pap.: Erdrosselt! (*Für sich:*) Bin in meinem Leben nicht so stark gewesen, als heute.
Die drei Damen (*erscheinen verschleiert. Sie drohen und rufen zugleich*): Papageno!
Pap.: Aha, das geht mich an!—(*zu Tamino:*) Sieh dich um, Freund!
Tam.: Wer sind diese Damen?
Pap.: Wer sie eigentlich sind, weiss ich selbst nicht. Ich weiss nur soviel, dass sie mir täglich meine Vögel abnehmen, und mir dafür Wein, Zuckerbrot und süsse Feigen bringen.
Tam.: Sie sind vermutlich sehr schön?
Pap.: Ich denke nicht!—Denn wenn sie schön wären, würden sie ihre Gesichter nicht bedecken.
Die 3 D. (*näher tretend, drohend*): Papageno!
Pap. (*beiseite, zu Tamino*): Sei still! Sie drohen mir schon. —(*Laut.*) Du fragst, ob sie schön sind, und ich kann dir darauf nichts antworten, als dass ich in meinem Leben nichts Reizenderes sah.—(*Für sich:*) Jetzt werden sie bald wieder gut werden.—
Die 3 D. (*noch näher tretend, drohender*): Papageno!
Pap. (*beiseite*): Was muss ich denn heute verbrochen haben, dass sie so aufgebracht wider mich sind?—(*Er überreicht den Vogelbauer. Laut:*) Hier, meine Schönen, übergeb ich meine Vögel.
1. D. (*reicht ihm ein Gefäss mit Wasser*): Dafür schickt dir unsere Fürstin heute zum ersten Mal, statt Wein, reines, klares Wasser.

Tam. (*steps in his way*): Hey, there!
Pap.: Who's there?
Tam.: Tell me who you are, my jolly friend.
Pap.: Who am I? (*To himself:*) Silly question! (*To Tamino:*) A man, like you. Suppose I asked you who you were?
Tam.: Then I would tell you that I am of noble blood.
Pap.: That's above me. You must explain yourself more clearly if you want me to understand you.
Tam.: My father is a king, who rules over many lands and peoples. That is why they call me "Prince"
Pap.: Lands? Peoples? Prince? Tell me, are there any lands and peoples beyond these mountains?
Tam.: Thousands and thousands.
Pap.: Perhaps I could do a little speculating there with my birds.
Tam.: What is this land called? Who rules it?
Pap.: I can't answer you that any more than I can tell you how I happened to come into this world.
Tam. (*laughs*): What? Do you mean to tell me that you do not know where you were born, or who your parents were?
Pap.: Not a word! I only know that not far from here is my straw hut, which protects me from the cold and rain.
Tam.: But by what do you live?
Pap.: By eating and drinking, just as everyone else does.
Tam.: How do you get it?
Pap.: By exchange. I catch all kinds of birds for the star-flaming Queen and her ladies. In return, I receive food and drink every day from them.
Tam. (*to himself*): Star-flaming Queen? (*To Papageno:*) Tell me, good friend, were you ever fortunate enough to see this Goddess of the Night?
Pap.: See her? See the star-flaming Queen? What mortal can boast of ever having seen her? (*To himself:*) The way he stares at me! Pretty soon I shall begin to be afraid of him. (*To Tamino:*) Why do you stare at me so suspiciously?
Tam.: Well, I—I was wondering whether you are a human being or not.
Pap.: What was that?
Tam.: Considering those feathers covering you, you look rather—(*approaches him.*)
Pap.: Not like a bird, by any means? Stay away from me, I tell you, and don't trust me, because I have the strength of a giant. (*To himself:*) If he doesn't begin to be afraid of me soon, I shall have to run for it.
Tam.: Strength of a giant? (*Looks at the serpent.*) Then perhaps it was you who saved me, and fought this poisonous snake?
Pap.: Snake? (*Trembling, draws back a few steps.*) Is it dead or alive?
Tam.: But tell me, friend, how in the world did you ever fight this monster? You have no weapons!
Pap. (*has mastered himself again*): I don't need weapons. A good squeeze of my hand is more than weapons.

Tam.: Then you choked it?
Pap.: Choked it. (*To himself:*) Never in my life was I so strong as I am today.
The Three Ladies (*appear, veiled. In a menacing tone*): Papageno!
Pap.: Ah, that's for me! (*To Tamino:*) Turn around, friend!
Tam.: Who are these ladies?
Pap.: Who they actually are, I do not know myself. I only know this much: each day they take in my birds, and give me wine, sugar-bread, and sweet figs in return.
Tam.: I suppose they are very beautiful?
Pap.: I don't think so, for if they were, they would not have to cover up their faces.
The 3 L. (*coming nearer, menacingly*): Papageno!
Pap. (*aside to Tamino*): Wait a minute. Now they are after me. (*Aloud:*) You asked me whether these ladies are beautiful, and I can only say that never in my life have I seen anyone more charming. (*Aside:*) Now I guess that will put them in a good humor again.
The 3 L. (*still nearer, and more menacingly*): Pa-page-no!!!
Pap. (*aside*): Heavens, what can I have done today to have made them so angry? (*He hands them the cage. Aloud:*) Here, lovely ladies, I have brought you my birds.
1st L. (*gives him a jug of water*): This time, in return, the Queen sends you, instead of wine,—pure, clear water.

2. D.: Und mir befahl sie, dass ich, statt Zuckerbrot, diesen Stein dir überbringen soll. (*Sie überreicht Papageno den Stein.*) Ich wünsche, dass er dir wohlbekommen möge.

Pap.: Was? Steine soll ich fressen?

3. D.: Und statt der süssen Feigen, hab ich die Ehre, dir dies goldene Schloss vor den Mund zu schlagen. (*Sie hängt ihm das Schloss vor den Mund. Papageno zeigt seinen Schmerz durch Gebärden.*)

1. D.: Du willst vermutlich wissen, warum die Fürstin dich heute so wunderbar bestraft? (*Papageno bejaht es durch Nicken mit dem Kopf.*)

2. D.: Damit du künftig nie mehr Fremde belügst.

3. D.: Und dass du nie dich der Heldentaten rühmest, die andre vollzogen.

1. D.: Sag an, hast du diese Schlange bekämpft? (*Papageno verneint es durch Schütteln mit dem Kopf.*)

2. D.: Wer denn also? (*Papageno deutet an, dass er es nicht weiss.*)

3. D.: Wir waren's, Jüngling, die dich befreiten.—Hier, dies Gemälde schickt dir die grosse Fürstin: es ist das Bildnis ihrer Tochter. (*Sie überreicht es.*) Findest du, sagte sie, dass diese Züge dir nicht gleichgültig sind, dann ist Glück, Ehr und Ruhm dein Los!—Auf Wiedersehen. (*Geht ab.*)

2. D.: Adieu, Monsieur Papageno! (*Geht ab.*)

1. D.: Fein nicht zu hastig getrunken! (*Geht lachend ab. Papageno eilt in stummer Verlegenheit ab. Tamino hat gleich beim Empfange des Bildes seine Aufmerksamkeit nur diesem zugewendet.*)

2nd L.: And she ordered me, instead of sugar-bread, to give you this stone. (*Gives him the stone.*) Here's good health to you!

Pap.: What, I shall eat stones?

3rd L.: And instead of sweet figs, I have the honor of locking up your mouth with this golden padlock. (*Does so. Papageno shows his pain through gestures.*)

1st L.: I imagine you would like to know why the Queen punishes you in such a strange way? (*Papageno nods yes.*)

2nd L.: So that in the future you will never again tell lies to strangers!

3rd L.: And that you will never boast of heroic deeds achieved by others.

1st L.: Tell us, did *you* kill this serpent? (*Papageno shakes his head.*)

2nd L.? Who did, then? (*Papageno shrugs his shoulders.*)

3rd L.: Prince, it was we who saved you. The great Queen sends you this portrait of her daughter. (*Hands it to him.*) If you find that these features are not indifferent to you, she says, then happiness, honor, and glory will be your destiny. Farewell. (*Exit.*)

2nd L.: Adieu, Monsieur Papageno! (*Exit*)

1st L.: Don't drink too fast! (*Exit, laughing. Exit Papageno, who has continued to pantomime. Tamino has not taken his eyes off the picture since he received it.*)

No. 3. Aria

Et - was kann ich zwar nicht nennen; doch fühl ich's hier wie Feu - er brennen.
can - not name this strange de - sire Which burns my heart with glowing fire

Soll die Emp-fin - dung Lie-be sein? Soll die Emp-fin - dung Lie-be sein?
Can this e - mo - tion love reveal? Can this e - mo - tion love re-veal?

Ja, ja! Die Lie-be ist's al - lein, die Lie-be, die Lie-be, die Lie be
Ah yes! 'Tis love alone I feel, 'tis love, 'tis love, 'tis love,

ist's al - lein. O wenn ich sie nur fin - den
Love a - lone! Oh, how to see her I am

könn - te! o wenn sie doch schon vor mir stän - de! Ich wür - de,
yearn - ing! Oh, how to find her I am burn - ing! I would then,

1. D.: Rüste dich mit Mut und Standhaftigkeit, schöner Jüngling!—Die Fürstin—
2. D.: hat mir aufgetragen, dir zu sagen—
3. D.: dass der Weg zu deinem künftigen Glücke nunmehr gebahnt sei.
1. D.: Sie hat jedes deiner Worte gehört;—sie hat—
2. D.: jeden Zug in deinem Gesichte gelesen,—
3. D.: hat beschlossen, dich ganz glücklich zu machen.—Hat dieser Jüngling, sprach sie, auch so viel Mut und Tapferkeit, als er zärtlich ist, o, so ist meine Tochter ganz gewiss gerettet.
Tam.: Kommt, Mädchen, führt mich!—Sie sei gerettet! Das schwöre ich bei meiner Liebe, bei meinem Herzen! (*Kurzer starker Donner.*) Ihr Götter, was ist das? (*Es wird dunkel.*)
Die 3 D.: Fasse dich!
1. D.: Es verkündet die Ankunft unserer Königin. (*Donner.*)
Die 3 D.: Sie kommt!—(*Donner.*) Sie kommt!—(*Donner.*) Sie kommt!—(*Donner. Die Berge teilen sich, man erblickt einen Sternenhimmel und den Thron der Königin der Nacht.*)

1st L.: Prepare yourself with courage and steadfastness, noble Prince, for the Queen—
2nd L.: bade me to tell you—
3rd L.: that the path to your future happiness now lies open to you.
1st L.: She has heard every word you said. She has—
2nd L.: read every expression of your features,—
3rd L.: decided to make you completely happy. "Oh, if this youth", said she, "is as zealous and brave as he is kind-hearted, then my daughter will certainly be saved!"
Tam.: Come, maidens, lead me. She shall be saved! I swear it by my love and by my heart. (*Short, loud thunder.*) Ye Gods! What is that? (*It becomes dark.*)
The 3 L.: Take heart!
First Lady: That betokens the arrival of our Queen. (*Thunder.*)
The 3 L.: She comes! (*Thunder.*) She comes! (*Thunder.*) She comes! (*Thunder. The mountains part; against a starry heaven the Queen of the Night's throne is revealed.*)

No. 4. Recitative and Aria

Aria
Larghetto

Mut-terherz zu trösten.
sor-row of a moth-er.

Zum Lei-den bin ich aus-er-ko-ren; denn mei-ne
In lone-ly grief I am for-sak-en, For my poor

Toch-ter feh-let mir. Durch sie ging all mein Glück ver-lo-ren, durch sie ging all mein Glück ver-
child no more I see.___ With her my hap-pi-ness was tak-en. With her my hap-pi-ness was

lo-ren, ein Bö-sewicht, ein Bö- - - sewicht entfloh mit
tak-en; An e-vil fiend, an e- - - vil fiend tore her from

ihr. Noch seh ich ihr Zittern mit ban-gem Er-
me. How help-less she cow-ered, Her strength o-ver-

schüttern, ihr ängst-li-ches Be-ben, ihr schüch-ter-nes
pow-ered! What sad con-ster-na-tion! What vain des-per-

Streben! Ich muß-te sie mir rau-ben se-hen. Ach helft! ach helft! war alles, was sie
a-tion! With nameless woe my heart was bleed-ing. "Ah help, ah help!" was all I heard her

sprach; al-lein ver-ge-bens war ihr Fle-hen, denn mei-ne Hül-fe war zu schwach,
speak. How-ev-er, fu-tile was her plead-ing, For all my ef-fort was too weak,

Allegro moderato

denn mei-ne Hül-fe, mei-ne Hül-fe war zu schwach.
For all my ef-forts, all my ef-forts were too weak.

Du, du, du wirst sie zu be-frei-en ge - hen,
You, you, you shall free her from bonds of slav - 'ry!

du wirst der Toch - ter Ret - ter sein, ja, du wirst der
You shall re - lease this child of mine, Yes, you shall re -

Toch - ter Ret - ter sein! Und werd ich dich als Sie - ger
lease this child of mine! And to re - ward you for your

se - hen, so sei sie dann auf e - wig dein, so sei sie dann
brav - 'ry, For-ev-er then she shall be thine, For-ev-er then

cresc. fp

auf
for-

e - - - - - - - wig dein, auf e - wig
ev - - - - - - er thine. for ev - er

cresc.

dein, auf e - wig dein! *(She steps back. Thunder. The mountains close;*
thine, for ev - er thine! *it becomes light. Rocky landscape as before.)*

3

Tam. (*nach einer Pause*): Ist's denn auch Wirklichkeit,
was ich sah?—O ihr guten Götter, täuscht mich nicht.
(*Er will sich entfernen, Papageno tritt ihm in den Weg.*)

Tam. (*after pause*): Was it reality I saw? O good Gods,
do not deceive me! (*He tarts to leave, but Papageno steps
in his path.*)

No. 5. Quintet

34

1st Lady *(gives Tamino*

bestände Lieb und Bru-der-bund. O Prinz, nimm
Would yield to broth-er-hood and right. O Prince, up-

bestände Lieb und Bru-der-bund.
Would yield to broth-er-hood and right.

bestände Lieb und Bru-der-bund.
Would yield to broth-er-hood and right.

bestände Lieb und Bru-der-bund.
Would yield to broth-er-hood and right.

a golden flute)

dies Ge-schenk von mir, dies sen-det uns-re Für-stin dir.
on our Queen's command,— We lay this trea-sure in your hand.

Die Zau-ber-flö-te wird dich schützen, im größ-ten Unglück un-ter-
This mag-ic flute she deigns to send you. Its mys-tic mu-sic will de-

1st & 2nd L.

stützen. Hie-mit kannst du allmächtig handeln, der Men-schen Leidenschaft ver-wandeln, der
fend you. And when this pow-er is as-sert-ed, All hu-man pas-sions are con-vert-ed; The

3rd L.

Hie-mit kannst du allmächtig handeln, der Men-schen Leidenschaft ver-wandeln, der
And when this pow-er is as-sert-ed, All hu-man pas-sions are con-vert-ed; The

3 Ladies

fehl ich mich. Dich emp - feh - len kannst du im - mer, doch be - stimmt die Für - stin
lib - er - ty? No, to more im - por - tant du - ties Our_ Queen has or - dered

dich, mit dem Prin - zen ohn Ver - wei - len, nach Sa - ra - stros Burg zu
you. To Sa - ra - stro's tem - ple yon - der, With the Prince you are to

Papageno

ei - len. Nein! da - für be - dank ich mich! Von euch sel - ber hör - te ich, daß er
wan - der. No, my ladies, thank you, no! You yourselves have told me so: That he's

wie ein Ti - ger - tier; si - cher ließ ohn al - le Gnaden mich Sa - ra - stro rupfen,
sav - age as a boar, I am sure that he would roast me, Fry and toast me, fry and

3 Ladies

bra - ten, rupfen, bra - ten, rupfen, bra - ten, setz - te mich den Hun - den für:
toast me, fry and toast me, fry and toast me, Noth - ing less and noth - ing more!

Dich schützt der
The Prince will

cresc. f p cresc. f fp

Prinz, trau ihm al - lein! da-für sollst du sein Die - ner sein. Daß doch der
shield you, have no fear; You will be safe while he is near. Oh, would the

Prinz beim Teu - fel wä - re! Mein Le - ben ist mir lieb, am En - de
dev - il on - ly take him! My life I rate too high. He'll steal a-

schleicht, bei mei - ner Eh - re. er von mir wie ein Dieb.
way, up - on my hon - or, Like a thief on the sly!

1st Lady *(hands Papageno a little box containing bells)* Papageno

Hier nimm dies Klei-nod, es ist dein. Ei! ei! was mag dar-
This pre - cious case is meant for you. Well! well! and may I

3 Ladies   Papageno

innen sein? Dar-in-nen hörst du Glöckchen tö - nen. Werd ich sie auch wohl spie-len
see it too? Here - in are bells of sil-ver swing-ing. But shall I learn to set them

wie man die Burg / wohl fin - den
Who will as guide / show us the

Burg wohl finden kann? / wie man die Burg / wohl fin - den
guide show us the way, / Who will as guide / show us the

Andante

kann, wie man die Burg wohl fin - den kann?
way, Who will as guide show us the way?

kann, wie man die Burg wohl fin - den kann?
way, Who will as guide show us the way?

Andante

p dolce.

(The Three Ladies return.)

1st & 2nd L.

sotto voce

Drei Knäbchen, jung, schön, hold und weise, um-schweben euch auf
3rd Lady Three spir - its young and wise will guide you And on your jour - ney

Drei Knäbchen, jung, schön, hold und weise, um-schweben euch auf
Three spir - its young and wise will guide you And on your jour - ney

eu - rer Rei - se, sie wer - den eu - re Füh - rer sein, folgt ihrem Ra - te
stay be - side you. Re - ly on them where they may lead. On - ly their counsel

eu - rer Rei - se, sie wer - den eu - re Füh - rer sein, folgt ihrem Ra - te
stay be - side you. Re - ly on them where they may lead. On - ly their counsel

mf   p

Wie-dersehn, / fare you well. auf Wieder-sehn. / so fare you well! (Exeunt.)

auf Wiedersehn, / So fareyouwell, auf Wiedersehn. / so fareyouwell! (Exit.)

auf Wiedersehn, / So fareyouwell, auf Wiedersehn. / so fareyouwell! (Exit.)

(Verwandlung. Ein prächtiges ägyptisches Zimmer. Zwei Sklaven tragen schöne Polster nebst einem prächtigen, türkischen Tisch heraus, breiten Teppiche auf; sodann kommt der dritte Sklave.)

3. Sklave: Hahaha!
1. Sklave: Pst! Pst!
2. Sklave: Was soll denn das Lachen?
3. S.: Unser Peiniger, der alles belauschende Mohr wird morgen sicherlich gehangen oder gespiesst.—Pamina!—Hahaha!
1. S.: Nun?
3. S.: Das reizende Mädchen!—Hahaha!
2. S.: Nun?
3. S.: Ist entsprungen.
1. u. 2. S.: Entsprungen?
1. S.: Und sie entkam?
3. S.: Unfehlbar!—Wenigstens ist's mein wahrer Wunsch.
1. S.: O, Dank euch, ihr guten Götter! Ihr habt meine Bitte erhört.
3. S.: Sagt' ich euch nicht immer, es wird doch ein Tag für uns scheinen, wo wir gerochen, und der schwarze Monostatos bestraft werden wird?
2. S.: Was spricht nun der Mohr zu der Geschichte?
1. S.: Er weiss doch davon?
3. S.: Natürlich! Sie entlief vor seinen Augen.—Wie mir einige Brüder erzählten, die im Garten arbeiteten und von weitem sahen und hörten, so ist der Mohr nicht mehr zu retten; auch wenn Pamina von Sarastros Gefolge wieder eingebracht würde.
1. u. 2. S.: Wieso?
3. S.: Du kennst ja den üppigen Wanst und seine Weise; das Mädchen aber war klüger, als ich dachte.—In dem Augenblicke, als er zu siegen glaubte, rief sie Sarastros Namen: das erschütterte den Mohren; er blieb stumm und unbeweglich stehen.—Indes lief Pamina nach dem Kanal und schiffte von selbst in einer Gondel dem Palmenwäldchen zu.
1. S.: O, wie wird das schüchterne Reh mit Todesangst dem Palast ihrer zärtlichen Mutter zueilen!
Monostatos (von innen): He, Sklaven!
1. S.: Monostatos' Stimme!
Mon.: He, Sklaven! Schafft Fesseln herbei!
Die 3 S.: Fesseln?
1. S. (läuft zur Seitentür): Doch nicht für Pamina? O ihr Götter! Da seht, Brüder, das Mädchen ist gefangen.
2. u. 3. S.: Pamina?—Schrecklicher Anblick!
1. S.: Seht, wie der unbarmherzige Teufel sie bei ihren zarten Händchen fasst—das halt ich nicht aus. (Geht auf die andere Seite ab.)
2. S.: Ich noch weniger.—(Auch dort ab.)
3. S.: So was sehen zu müssen ist Höllenmarter! (Ab.)

(Change of scene. Elaborate Egyptian room. Two Slaves bring embroidered pillows and a beautiful Turkish table; they spread out rugs; then the Third Slave appears.)

3rd Slave: Ha! ha! ha!
1st Slave: Sh! sh!
2nd Slave: What is the meaning of that laughter?
3rd S.: Our torturer, the ever-spying Moor, will surely be hung or put on the rack tomorrow.—Pamina! Ha! ha!
1st S.: Well?
3rd S.: The beautiful maiden—ha! ha! ha!
2nd S.: Well?
3rd S.: has run away.
1st & 2nd S.: Run away?
1st S.: And she escaped?
3rd S.: Without doubt! At least it is my sincere wish.
1st S.: Oh, thank you, good Gods! You have heard my plea!
3rd S.: Did I not always tell you that there would come a day for us when we will be avenged, and the black Monostatos will be punished?
2nd S.: What does the Moor say to all this?
1st S.: He knows about it, does he not?
3rd S.: Naturally! She escaped before his very eyes! As some brothers told me, who were working in the garden and who listened and watched from the distance, the Moor no longer can be saved, even if Pamina should be brought back again by Sarastro's suite.
1st & 2nd S.: How so?
3rd S.: You know the old thick-paunch and his ways. The maiden was more clever, however, than I thought. At the moment when he believed he had won, she called Sarastro's name. That terrified the Moor. He stood silent and motionless. Meanwhile Pamina ran to the canal and floated, driven by the stream, in a gondola towards the palm grove.
1st S.: Oh, how the shy deer will hurry, frightened to death, to the palace of her mother!
Monostatos (offstage): Ho, Slaves!
1st S.: Monostatos's voice!
Mon.: Ho, Slaves! Bring chains!
3 Slaves: Chains?
1st S. (runs to the side door): Not for Pamina! Oh, Heavens! Look there, brothers! The maiden has been caught!
2nd & 3rd S.: Pamina?—Horrible sight!
1st S.: See how the relentless devil grasps her by her tender hands—I cannot bear it! (Exit, at the other side.)
2nd S.: Even less can I. (Exit by the same way.)
3rd S.: To have to see such a thing is the torture of hell! (Exit.)

No. 6. Trio

48

laß mich lie - ber sterben, weil nichts, Bar - - bar!_____ dich rühren
beg you, rath - er slay me, If naught __ can __ stir _____ your e - vil

(She sinks, unconscious, on a sofa.)

Monostatos

(Exeunt Slaves.)

kann. Nun fort! nun fort! laßt mich bei ihr al - lein.
heart. Get out, get out! Leave me a - lone with her!

(outside, at the window) (Monostatos does not notice him.)

Papageno

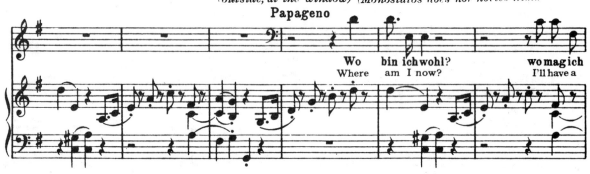

Wo bin ich wohl? wo mag ich
Where am I now? I'll have a

sein? A - ha! da find ich Leute. Ge-wagt! ich geh hin-ein. (Enter.)
glance. A - ha! there are some people. All right, I'll take a chance.

Pam. (*spricht wie im Traum*): Mutter—Mutter—Mutter! (*Sie erholt sich, sieht sich um.*) Wie?—Noch schlägt dies Herz?—Zu neuen Qualen erwacht?—O, das ist hart, sehr hart!—Mir bitterer, als der Tod. (*Papageno tritt ein.*)

Pap.: Bin ich nicht ein Narr, dass ich mich schrecken liess?—Es gibt ja schwarze Vögel in der Welt, warum denn nicht auch schwarze Menschen?—(*Er erblickt Pamina.*) Ah, sieh da! Hier ist das schöne Mädchen noch.—Du Tochter der nächtlichen Königin—

Pam. (*erhebt sich*): Nächtliche Königin?—Wer bist du?

Pap.: Ein Abgesandter der sternflammenden Königin.

Pam. (*freudig*): Meiner Mutter?—O Wonne!—Dein Name?

Pap.: Papageno.

Pam.: Papageno?—Papageno—ich erinnere mich, den Namen oft gehört zu haben, dich selbst aber sah ich nie.

Pap.: Ich dich ebensowenig.

Pam.: Du kennst also meine gute, zärtliche Mutter?

Pap.: Wenn du die Tochter der nächtlichen Königin bist —ja!

Pam.: O, ich bin es.

Pap.: Das will ich gleich erkennen. (*Er sieht das Portrait an, welches der Prinz zuvor empfangen, und das Papageno nun an einem Band am Halse trägt.*) Die Augen schwarz—richtig, schwarz.—Die Lippen rot—richtig, rot.—Blonde Haare—blonde Haare.—Alles trifft ein, bis auf Händ und Füsse.——Nach dem Gemälde zu schliessen, sollst du weder Hände noch Füsse haben; denn hier sind keine angezeigt.

Pam.: Erlaube mir—Ja, ich bin's!—Wie kam es in deine Hände?

Pap.: Ich muss dir das umständlicher erzählen.—Ich kam heute früh, wie gewöhnlich, zu deiner Mutter Palast mit meiner Lieferung—

Pam.: Lieferung?

Pap.: Ja, ich liefere deiner Mutter und ihren Jungfrauen schon seit vielen Jahren alle die schönen Vögel in den Palast.—Eben als ich im Begriff war, meine Vögel abzugeben, sah ich einen Menschen vor mir, der sich Prinz nennen lässt.—Dieser Prinz hat deine Mutter so eingenommen, dass sie ihm dein Bildnis schenkte und ihm befahl, dich zu befreien.—Sein Entschluss war so schnell, als seine Liebe zu dir.

Pam.: Liebe? (*Freudig.*) Er liebt mich also? O, sage mir das noch einmal, ich höre das Wort Liebe gar zu gern.

Pap.: Das glaube ich dir, du bist ja ein Mädchen.—Wo blieb ich denn?

Pam.: Bei der Liebe.

Pap.: Richtig, bei der Liebe! Das nenn ich ein Gedächtnis haben! Komm, du wirst Augen machen, wenn du den schönen Jüngling erblickst.

Pam.: Wohl denn, es sei gewagt! (*Sie gehen, Pamina kehrt um.*) Aber wenn dies ein Fallstrick wäre—wenn dieser nun ein böser Geist von Sarastros Gefolge wäre?— (*Sieht ihn bedenklich an.*)

Pap.: Ich ein böser Geist?—Wo denkst du hin.—Ich bin der beste Geist von der Welt.

Pam.: Vergib, vergib, wenn ich dich beleidigte! Du hast ein gefühlvolles Herz.

Pap.: Ach, freilich habe ich ein gefühlvolles Herz! Aber was nützt mir das alles?—Ich möchte mir oft alle meine Federn ausrupfen, wenn ich bedenke, dass Papageno noch keine Papagena hat.

Pam.: Armer Mann! Du hast also noch kein Weib?

Pap.: Noch nicht einmal ein Mädchen, viel weniger ein Weib!—Und unsereiner hat doch auch bisweilen seine lustigen Stunden, wo man gern gesellschaftliche Unterhaltung haben möchte.

Pam.: Geduld, Freund! Der Himmel wird auch für dich sorgen; er wird dir eine Freundin schicken, ehe du dir's vermutest.

Pap.: Wenn er sie nur bald schickte!

Pam. (*speaks as if in a dream*): Mother! Mother! Mother! (*She recovers, looks around.*) What, my heart still beats? Am I still alive? Do I wake to new troubles? Oh, that is hard, very hard! This is more bitter to me than death! (*Papageno enters again.*)

Pap.: Wasn't I a fool to be frightened? There are black birds in the world, so why not black people? Ah, see there! Here is the lovely maiden. You, daughter of the Queen of the Night—

Pam. (*rises*): Queen of the Night? Who are you?

Pap.: A messenger of the star-flaming Queen.

Pam. (*joyfully*): My mother? O Joy! Your name?

Pap.: Papageno.

Pam.: Papageno? Papageno—I remember having heard your name often, but you yourself I never saw.

Pap.: Nor I you.

Pam.: Then you know my good, loving mother?

Pap.: If you are the daughter of the Queen of the Night, —yes.

Pam.: Yes, I am.

Pap.: I'll soon find out. (*He looks at the portrait which previously had been given to the Prince and which Papageno now wears around his neck on a ribbon.*) Eyes black— right—black. Lips red—right—red. Blond hair— blond hair. Everything is correct, except the hands and feet; because, judging from this picture, you haven't any hands and feet, for none are painted here.

Pam.: Let me see. Yes, it is my portrait, but how did it come into your hands?

Pap.: To tell you that will be a longer story. I went, early this morning, as usual, to your mother's palace, to make my delivery.

Pam.: Delivery?

Pap.: Yes, for years I have delivered all the finest birds I could catch to your mother and her ladies, at the palace. Just as I was about to hand over the birds, I saw someone standing in front of me who called himself "Prince". This prince so impressed your mother that she gave him your portrait, and ordered him to set you free. His decision was just as quick as his love for you.

Pam. (*joyfully*): Love? He loves me, then? Oh, say that again! It feels so good to hear the word "love"!

Pap.: That I believe, for you are a girl. But where was I then?

Pam.: You said "love".

Pap.: Right, love. That's what I call memory! Come, your eyes will be bright when you see the handsome youth.

Pam.: Well then, let us go. (*They start to go; Pamina turns around.*) But suppose this is only a trap? Suppose you are but an evil genius of Sarastro? (*She looks at him doubtfully.*)

Pap.: I? An evil genius? What are you thinking of? I am no genius at all.

Pam.: Friend, forgive me if I have offended you. You have a tender heart.

Pap.: Ah, certainly I have a tender heart! But what good does it do me? Sometimes I feel like ripping out all my feathers when I think that Papageno hasn't found a Papagena yet.

Pam.: Poor man! Then you have no wife?

Pap.: Not even a girl, let alone a wife! And people like us have their gay hours, too, when they would like to have some fun.

Pam.: Have patience, friend. The gods will take care of you. They will send you a wife, before you even think.

Pap.: If they would only send her soon!

No. 7. Duet

Weib, und Weib und Mann rei - chen an die Gott - heit an,
man, and man and wife, Reach the height of god - ly life,

Weib, und Weib und Mann rei - chen an die Gott - heit an,
man, and man and wife, Reach the height of god - ly life,

an die Gottheit an, an die Gottheit an. (Exit.)
of a god - ly life, of a god - ly life.

an die Gottheit an, an die Gottheit an. (Exit.)
of a god - ly life, of a god - ly life.

(Change of scene. A grove, in the middle of which stand three temples.)

No. 8. Finale

Larghetto

(The Three Spirits lead Tamino in.)

1st & 2nd Spirits

Zum Zie - le führt dich die - se Bahn, doch
Your journey's end you soon will reach; Yet

3rd Spirit

Zum Zie - le führt dich die - se Bahn, doch
Your journey's end you soon will reach; Yet

mußt du, Jüngling, männlich sie - gen. Drum hö-re uns-re Leh-re an: Sei standhaft, duldsam und ver-
win you must by man-ly dar - ing: But hark-en to these words we teach: Be si-lent, steadfast, and for-

mußt du, Jüngling, männlich sie - gen. Drum hö-re uns-re Leh-re an: Sei standhaft, duldsam und ver-
win you must by man-ly dar - ing; But hark-en to these words we teach: Be si-lent, steadfast, and for-

ten.   ten.

schwiegen. **Tamino** *(has hung his flute around his neck)*
bear-ing.

schwiegen. Ihr holden Klei - nen sagt mir an,   ob ich Pa - mi - nen ret - ten
bear-ing. Ye kind-ly spir - its, tell   me, please,   May I Pa - mi - na soon re-

ten.

1st & 2nd Spirits

Dies kund - zu-tun, steht uns nicht an: Sei standhaft,   duldsam   und ver-
3rd Spirit To   an-swer this we're not al-lowed; Be   si-lent,   steadfast,   and for-

kann?   Dies kund - zu-tun, steht uns nicht an: Sei standhaft,   duldsam   und ver-
lease?   To   an-swer this we're not al-lowed; Be   si-lent,   steadfast,   and for-

ten.   ten.

schwiegen. Be - den-ke dies,   kurz, sei ein Mann! Dann, Jüngling, wirst _____ du männlich
bear-ing! Have cour-age, Prince, brave be and proud. Then you will win _____ by man - ly

schwiegen. Be - den-ke dies,   kurz, sei ein Mann!   Dann, Jüngling, wirst du männlich
bear-ing! Have cour-age, Prince, brave be and proud.   Then you will win   by man - ly

ten.

sie - gen, dann, Jüngling, wirst du männlich sie - gen. *(Exit.)*
dar - ing, Then you will win by man-ly dar - ing.

sie - gen, dann, Jüngling, wirst du männlich sie - gen. *(Exeunt.)*
dar - ing, Then you will win by man-ly dar - ing.

Tamino *Recit.*

Die Weisheitslehre dieser Knaben sei e-wig
These words of wisdom tru-ly spo-ken Be in my

p

mir ins Herz gegraben. Wo bin ich nun? was wird mit mir? Ist dies der Sitz der
heart engraved as to-ken. Where am I now? What will be-tide? Do here the might-y

fp

Göt - ter hier? Es zei-gen die Pfor-ten, es zei-gen die Säu-len,
gods a-bide? These arch-es and por-tals, mys-te-ri-ous dwell-ing,

daß Klug-heit und Ar-beit und Kün-ste hier
Of rea-son, and la-bor, and arts are fore-

Priest

tum. Die Worte sind von hohem Sinn, al-lein, wie willst du diese fin-den? Dich lei-tet
seek. These words a loft-y mind be-speak. And yet, how do you hope to earn them? Not love nor

a tempo Adagio

Tamino

Lieb und Tu-gend nicht, weil Tod und Ra-che dich ent-zün-den. Nur Ra-che für den
vir-tue do you heed; With death and ven-geance you are burn-ing. Yes, vengeance for a

Adagio

cresc. *f* *Recit.*

Priest **Tamino** *(quickly)*

Bö-sewicht! Den wirst du wohl bei uns nicht fin-den. Sa-ra-stro herrscht in die-sen
vil-lain's deed! My son, you are ensnared in er-ror. Is this Sa-ra-stro's realm of

p

Priest **Tamino** *(quickly)* **Priest** *(slowly)*

Gründen? Ja! ja! Sa-rastro herrschet hier. Doch in dem Weisheitstempel nicht? Er herrscht im
ter-ror? 'Tis true! Sa-ra-stro is our lord. But not in wisdom's tem-ple, too? He rules in

ff

Tamino *(wishes to go)* **Priest**

Weisheitstempel hier. So ist denn al--les Heuche-lei! Willst du schon wieder gehn?
wisdom's temple, too. Then all is false __ as false can be! You mean to leave us then?

f *p*

Tamino
Ja, ich will gehn, froh und frei, nie eu-ren Tempel sehn.
Yes, I will leave, glad and free, Nev-er re-turn a-gain.

Priest
Erklär dich nä-her mir, dich täuschet ein Be-trug.
Do not act hast-i-ly. You have been told a lie.

Tamino
Sa-ra-stro wohnet hier? das ist mir schon genug.
Sa-ra-stro is our lord, And that will do for me!

Priest
Wenn du dein Leben liebst, so re-de: bleibe da! Sa-rastro hassest du?
If you don't want to die, Give answer; do not go! You hate Sa-ra-stro so?

Tamino
Ich haß ihn ewig, ja!
Now and for-ev-er-more!

Priest
So gib mir dei-ne Gründe an.
Will you de-clare your reasons then.

Tamino
Er ist ein Unmensch, ein Ty-rann!
He is a ty-rant, foe of men!

Priest
Ist das, was du gesagt, er-wie-sen?
Have you for such a charge foundation?

Tamino
Durch ein unglücklich Weib bewiesen, das Gram und Jammer nie-der-
A woman, bowed by trib-u-la-tion, Who suf-fers anguished pain and

Andante
(plays the flute)

Wie stark ist nicht dein Zau - ber-ton! weil, hol - - de Flö - te, holde
How strong your tone with mag - ic spell, Dear flute,_____ is bind - ing. By your

(plays)

Flö - te durch____ dein Spie - len selbst wilde Tie-re Freu-de füh - len.
tone, dear flute,_____ each be - ing New hap-piness and joy is find - ing.

Wie stark ist nicht dein
How strong your tone with

Zau - ber-ton! weil hol - de
mag - ic spell! How strong your

66

68

Pamina
Ach, nun ist's mit uns vor-bei!
Now there is no more to hope!
Papageno
Ach, nun ist's mit uns vor-bei!
Now there is no more to hope!
Wer viel
Now it's
Monost.
bei!
rope!
He! ihr Sklaven, kommt her-bei!
Ho, you slaves, bring chains and rope!
(Enter slaves.)
Papageno
wagt, wer viel wagt, wer viel wagt, gewinnt oft viel. Komm, du schö-nes Glok-ken-
time, now it's time, now it's time to work the spell. Come, my love-ly mag-ic
(Papageno plays on his bells.)
spiel, laß die Glöckchen klingen, klingen, daß die Ohren ih-nen singen.
bell, Let your mel-o-dy be ringing. Save us by your magic singing!
(The slaves dance.)
Monostatos and Slaves
Ten.
Das klinget so herrlich, das klinget so schön! La la ra, la la
Bass
This jingles so soft-ly, this jingles so clear! La la ra, la la

(They withdraw, singing and dancing.)

wollte deiner Macht entfliehn. Al - lein die Schuld liegt nicht an mir. Der bö-se Mohr verlangte
tried es-cape from your do-main. A - las! the guilt falls not on me. The cru-el Moor wants me to

Lie - be, dar - um, o Herr! entfloh ich dir. Sarastro
love him; Therefore, my lord, I tried to flee.

Steh auf, er - heit - re dich, o
A - rise, con-sole your-self, Pa-

Lie - be! denn oh - ne erst in dich zu dringen, weiß ich von dei-nem Her-zen
mi - na! The name of your de-vot-ed lov-er I need not ask you to im-

mehr, du lie - best ei - nen an - dern sehr, ei - nen
part, I read the se-crets of your heart, all your

an - dern sehr. Zur Lie - be will ich dich nicht zwin-gen, doch geb ich dir die Frei - heit
se - cret heart. Through me you will not have to suf - fer, But yet I will not set you

Göt-tern gleich, den Göt - - - tern, den Göt-tern gleich, den

par - a - dise, Then earth _____ is a par - a - dise, Then

Göt - - - tern, den Göt - tern gleich, den Göt - tern gleich, den

earth _____ is a par - a - dise, a par - a - dise, a

Göt - tern gleich, den Göt - - tern gleich. (Sarastro

par - a - dise, a par - a - dise.

gives Pamina his hand and goes with her to the center portal.) *(Tamino and Papageno, guided*

by the Two Priests, turn to the exit.)

End of Act I

Act II
No. 9. March of the Priests
(Forest of palm trees)

Andante

sotto voce

(The Priests circle the stage in a festive procession, and take their places. At the end, Sarastro appears, ad-

vancing to a position in their midst.)

Adagio *(Three blasts on the horns, sounded by Priests)*

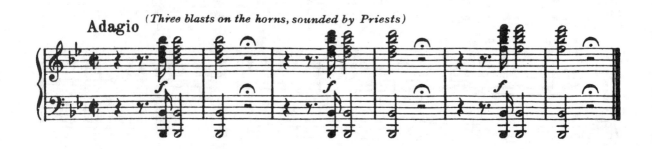

Sar.: Ihr, in dem Weisheitstempel eingeweihten Diener der grossen Götter Osiris und Isis!—Mit reiner Seele erklär ich euch, dass unsere heutige Versammlung eine der wichtigsten unserer Zeit ist.—Tamino, ein Königssohn, wandelt an der nördlichen Pforte unseres Tempels, und seufzt mit tugendvollem Herzen nach einem Gegenstand, den wir alle mit Mühe und Fleiss erringen müssen.—Diesen Tugendhaften zu bewachen, ihm freundschaftlich die Hand zu bieten, sei heute eine unserer wichtigsten Pflichten.

Erster Priester: Er besitzt Tugend?
Sar.: Tugend!
Zweiter Priester: Auch Verschwiegenheit?
Sar.: Verschwiegenheit!
Dritter Priester: Ist wohltätig?
Sar.: Wohltätig!—Haltet ihr ihn für würdig, so folgt meinem Beispiele. (*Sie blasen dreimal in die Hörner.*) Gerührt über die Einigkeit eurer Herzen, dankt Sarastro euch im Namen der Menschheit.—Pamina, das sanfte, tugendhafte Mädchen, haben die Götter dem holden Jünglinge bestimmt; dies ist der Grund, warum ich sie der stolzen Mutter entriss.—Das Weib dünkt sich gross zu sein, hofft durch Blendwerk und Aberglauben das Volk zu berücken und unsern festen Tempelbau zu zerstören. Allein, das soll sie nicht! Tamino, der holde Jüngling selbst, soll ihn mit uns befestigen und als Eingeweihter der Tugend Lohn, dem Laster aber Strafe sein. (*Der dreimalige Accord mit den Hörnern wird wiederholt.*)
Sprecher: Grosser Sarastro, deine weisheitsvollen Reden erkennen und bewundern wir; allein, wird Tamino auch die harten Prüfungen, so seiner warten, bekämpfen?—Er ist Prinz.
Sar.: Noch mehr—er ist Mensch!
Sprecher: Wenn er nun aber in seiner frühen Jugend leblos erblasste?
Sar.: Dann ist er Osiris und Isis gegeben, und wird der Götter Freuden früher fühlen, als wir. (*Der dreimalige Accord wird wiederholt.*) Man führe Tamino mit seinem Reisegefährten in den Vorhof des Tempels ein. (*Zum Sprecher, der vor ihm niederkniet.*) Und du, Freund, vollziehe dein heiliges Amt und lehre sie die Macht der Götter erkennen! (*Sprecher geht mit dem zweiten Priester ab.*)

Sar.: Consecrated servants of the great gods Osiris and Isis in the Temple of Wisdom, with pure heart I declare that today's assembly is one of the most important of our time. Tamino, a prince, waits at the northern portal of our temple, longing with a virtuous soul for the enlightenment towards which all of us have been striving with energy and zeal. To watch over this high-minded youth, and to extend to him the hand of friendship, will be one of our foremost duties this day.
First Priest: He is virtuous?
Sar.: Virtuous.
Second Priest: Can he keep silence?
Sar.: He can.
Third Priest: Is he benevolent?
Sar.: Benevolent. If you consider him worthy, follow my example. (*They blow three times on their horns.*) Moved by the unanimity of your hearts, Sarastro thanks you in the name of all mankind. Pamina, the gentle, virtuous maiden, has been designated by the gods for this noble youth; therefore I have torn her from the side of her proud mother. This woman considers herself great, and hopes through delusion and superstition to beguile the populace and to destroy the firm foundations of our temples. However, in that she shall not succeed. Tamino himself shall become one of us, and aid us to strengthen the power of virtue and wisdom. (*The three blasts on the horns are repeated.*)
Speaker: Great Sarastro, we admire your wise discourse. However, will Tamino be able to contend against the hard ordeals that await him? He is a prince.
Sar.: More than that,—he is a man.
Speaker: What if now, in his early youth, he pales in death?
Sar.: Then he would experience the celestial joys of Osiris and Isis sooner than we. (*The three blasts on the horns are repeated.*) Let Tamino and his companions be led into the court of the temple, (*to the Speaker, who kneels before him:*) and you, friend, fulfil your holy office and teach to both what duty to humanity is; teach them to perceive the might of the gods. (*Exeunt Speaker and Second Priest.*)

No. 10. Aria and Chorus of the Priests

stärkt mit Ge - duld sie in Ge-fahr,
Lead them to find the path of right!

Ten. I. II.

Chorus of Priests

stärkt mit Ge - duld sie in Ge-fahr.

Bass I. II.

Lead them to find the path of right!

Laßt sie der Prü - fung Früchte sehen, doch sollen sie zu Gra - be gehen, so lohnt der
Let them be strong a - gainst temp-ta-tion; But if they fail in their pro - ba-tion, Do not their

Tu - gend küh - nen Lauf, nehmt sie in eu - ren Wohnsitz auf, nehmt sie in
vir - tue meed — de - ny. Take them to your a - bode on high, Take them to

eu - ren Wohnsitz auf,
your a - bode on high.

Chorus

nehmt sie in eu - ren Wohnsitz auf.

Take them to your a - bode on high.

(*Verwandlung. Kurzer Vorhof des Tempels. Es ist Nacht. Tamino und Papageno werden vom Sprecher und dem zwei-'en Priester hereingeführt. Die Priester lösen ihnen den Schleier ab und entfernen sich damit.*)

Tam.: Eine schreckliche Nacht!—Papageno, bist du noch bei mir?

Pap.: I, freilich!

Tam.: Wo denkst du, dass wir uns nun befinden?

Pap.: Wo? Ja, wenn's nicht finster wäre, wollt ich dir's schon sagen—aber so—(*Donnerschlag.*) O weh!—

Tam.: Was ist's?

Pap.: Mir wird nicht wohl bei der Sache!

Tam.: Du hast Furcht, wie ich höre.

Pap.: Furcht eben nicht, nur eiskalt läuft's mir über den Rücken. (*Starker Donnerschlag.*) O weh!

Tam.: Was soll's?

Pap.: Ich glaube, ich bekomme ein kleines Fieber.

Tam.: Pfui, Papageno! Sei ein Mann!

Pap.: Ich wollt, ich wär ein Mädchen! (*Ein sehr starker Donnerschlag.*) O! o! o! Das ist mein letzter Augenblick! (*Sprecher und der zweite Priester erscheinen mit Fackeln.*)

Sprecher: Ihr Fremdlinge, was sucht oder fordert ihr von uns? Was treibt euch an, in unsere Mauern zu dringen?

Tam.: Freundschaft und Liebe.

Sprecher: Bist du bereit, es mit deinem Leben zu erkämpfen?

Tam.: Ja!

Sprecher: Auch wenn Tod dein Los wäre?

Tam.: Ja!

Sprecher: Prinz, noch ist's Zeit zu weichen—einen Schritt weiter, und es ist zu spät.—

Tam.: Weisheitslehre sei mein Sieg; Pamina, das holde Mädchen, mein Lohn.

Sprecher: Du unterziehst dich jeder Prüfung?

Tam.: Jeder!

Sprecher: Reiche mir deine Hand!—(*Sie reichen sich die Hände.*) So!

Zweiter Priester (*zu Papageno*): Willst auch du dir Weisheitsliebe erkämpfen?

Pap.: Kämpfen ist meine Sache nicht.—Ich verlange auch im Grunde gar keine Weisheit. Ich bin so ein Naturmensch, der sich mit Schlaf, Speise und Trank begnügt; —und wenn es ja sein könnte, dass ich mir einmal ein schönes Weibchen fange—

2. Pr.: Die wirst du nie erhalten, wenn du nicht unseren Prüfungen unterziehst.

Pap.: Worin besteht diese Prüfung?

2. Pr.: Dich allen unseren Gesetzen zu unterwerfen, selbst den Tod nicht zu scheuen.

Pap.: Ich bleibe ledig.

2. Pr.: Wenn nun aber Sarastro dir ein Mädchen aufbewahrt hätte, das an Farbe und Kleidung dir ganz gleich wäre?

Pap.: Mir gleich? Ist sie jung?

2. Pr.: Jung und schön!

Pap.: Und heisst?

2. Pr.: Papagena.

Pap.: Wie? Pa—?

2. Pr.: Papagena!

Pap.: Papagena?—Die möcht ich aus blosser Neugierde sehen.

2. Pr.: Sehen kannst du sie!—

Pap.: Aber wenn ich sie gesehen habe, hernach muss ich sterben? (*Zweiter Priester macht eine zweifelnde Pantomime.*) Ja? Ich bleibe ledig!

2. Pr.: Sehen kannst du sie, aber bis zur verlaufnen Zeit kein Wort mit ihr sprechen. Wird dein Geist so viel Standhaftigkeit besitzen, deine Zunge in Schranken zu halten?

Pap.: O ja!

2. Pr.: Deine Hand! Du sollst sie sehen. (*Sie reichen sich die Hände.*)

Sprecher (*zu Tamino*): Auch dir, Prinz, legen die Götter ein heilsames Stillschweigen auf; ohne dieses seid ihr beide verloren.—Du wirst Pamina sehen, aber nicht sie sprechen dürfen; dies ist der Anfang eurer Prüfungszeit.

(*Change of scene. Court of the temple. It is night. Tamino and Papageno are led in by the Speaker and the Second Priest. The Priests remove their veils, and depart with them.*)

Tam.: What a horrible night! Papageno, are you still with me?

Pap.: Most certainly I am!

Tam.: Where do you think we are now?

Pap.: Where we are? Well, if it were not so dark, I might be able to tell you; but this way—(*Thunder.*) Help! Help!

Tam.: What is wrong?

Pap.: I don't feel quite at ease in this affair.

Tam.: You are afraid, I can see.

Pap.: Not afraid, really,—I just have ice-cold shivers up and down my spine. (*Loud thunder.*) Oh, heavens!

Tam.: What is it?

Pap.: I think I am getting a slight fever.

Tam.: Shame on you, Papageno, be a man!

Pap.: I wish I were a girl! (*Very loud thunder.*) Oh! Oh! Oh! My hour has come! (*Speaker and Second Priest appear with torches.*)

Speaker: Strangers, what do you seek from us? What prompts you to intrude upon our sanctuary?

Tam.: Friendship and love.

Speaker: Are you prepared to fight for these virtues at risk of your very life?

Tam.: I am.

Speaker: Even if death were your lot?

Tam.: Yes.

Speaker: Prince, there is still time to turn back. One step more and it will be too late!

Tam.: Wisdom will gain my victory; Pamina, the lovely maiden, will be my reward!

Speaker: Are you willing to undergo every one of the trials?

Tam.: Every one.

Speaker: Give me your hand. (*They clasp hands.*)

Second Priest (*to Papageno*): Will you, too, fight for the love of wisdom?

Pap.: Fighting is not exactly in my line. To be truthful, I don't demand any wisdom, either. I'm just a child of nature, who is satisfied with sleep, food, and drink. And if I once could catch a pretty little wife—

2nd Pr.: That you shall never do unless you undergo our trials.

Pap.: Of what do these trials consist?

2nd Pr.: You must subject yourself to all our laws, and not even fear death.

Pap.: I'll remain single.

2nd Pr.: But if Sarastro has already chosen a bride for you who resembles you in color and dress perfectly?

Pap.: Resembles me? Is she young?

2nd Pr.: Young and beautiful!

Pap.: And her name is?

2nd Pr.: Papagena.

Pap.: Pa—pa—?

2nd Pr.: Papagena.

Pap.: Papagena! I really would like to see her out of sheer curiosity.

2nd Pr.: See her you may—

Pap.: But after I have seen her, then will I have to die? (*Second Priest shrugs his shoulders.*) Yes? I'll remain single.

2nd Pr.: You may see her, but as yet you must not speak a single word to her. Will your mind have sufficient strength to control your tongue?

Pap.: Oh, yes!

2nd Pr.: Your hand! You shall see her! (*They clasp hands.*)

Speaker (*to Tamino*): On you, too, Prince, the gods impose a reverent silence. If you fail in this, you both are lost. You will see Pamina, but you must not speak to her. This is the beginning of your probation time.

Andante

No. 11. Duet

Two Priests

Bewahret euch vor Wei-ber-tücken: dies ist des Bun-des er-ste Pflicht! Manch weiser
Beware of wo-man's craft-y scheming: This is the Or-der's first com-mand! Man-y a

Mann ließ sich be-rücken, er fehlte, er fehlte, und versah sich's nicht; ver-las-sen sah er sich am
man, of wiles not dreaming, Was tempted, was tempted and could not withstand. But then he saw he was mis-

sotto voce

En-de, ver-gol-ten seine Treu mit Hohn! Ver-ge-bens rang er sei-ne Hände, Tod und Verzweiflung
tak-en, The truth he came to know too late. At last he found himself for-saken. Death and dam-na-tion

war sein Lohn, Tod und Verzweiflung war sein Lohn. *(Exeunt both Priests. It becomes dark.)*
were his fate, Death and dam-na-tion were his fate.

Pap.: He, Lichter her! Lichter her!—Das ist doch wunderlich, so oft einen die Herren verlassen, sieht man mit offenen Augen nichts.
Tam.: Ertrag es mit Geduld, und denke, es ist der Götter Wille. *(Die drei Damen erscheinen mit Fackeln.)*

Pap.: Hey! Lights! Lights! It is really strange: each time these gentlemen leave us, you cannot see your hand in front of your face!
Tam.: Bear it with patience,—remember, it is the will of the gods! *(The Three Ladies appear with torches.)*

No. 12. Quintet

Papageno *(falls to the ground)*

O weh! o weh! o weh!
A - las! a - las! a - las!

(Sprecher und Priester treten mit Schleiern und Fackeln ein.)
Sprecher: Heil dir, Jüngling! Dein standhaft männliches Betragen hat gesiegt. Wir wollen also mit reinem Herzen unsere Wanderschaft weiter fortsetzen. *(Er gibt ihm den Schleier um.)* So! Nun komm! *(Er geht mit Tamino ab.)*
Zweiter Priester: Was seh ich! Freund, stehe auf! Wie ist dir?
Pap.: Ich lieg in einer Ohnmacht!
2. Pr.: Auf! Sammle dich und sei ein Mann!
Papageno *(steht auf)*: Aber sagt mir nur, meine Herren, warum muss ich denn alle diese Qualen und Schrecken empfinden?—Wenn mir ja die Götter eine Papagena bestimmten, warum denn mit so viel Gefahren sie erringen?
2. Pr.: Diese neugierige Frage mag deine Vernunft dir beantworten. Komm! Meine Pflicht heischt, dich weiterzuführen. *(Er gibt ihm den Schleier um.)*
Pap.: Bei so einer ewigen Wanderschaft möcht einem wohl die Liebe auf immer vergehen. *(Zweiter Priester geht mit ihm ab.)*

(Verwandlung. Garten. Pamina schlafend auf dem Sitz unter den Rosen.)
Monostatos: Ha, da find ich ja die spröde Schöne! Welcher Mensch würde bei so einem Anblick kalt und unempfindlich bleiben? Das Feuer, das in mir glimmt, wird mich noch verzehen! *(Er sieht sich um.)* Wenn ich wüsste—dass ich so ganz allein und unbelauscht wäre—Ein Küsschen, dächte ich, liesse sich entschuldigen.

(Speaker and Priest enter, carrying veils and torches.)
Speaker: Hail to thee, Prince! Thy steadfast, manly bearing has gained a victory! Thus we wish, with purest heart, to continue our travels. *(Covers Tamino's head with a veil.)* Come, then! *(Exeunt Speaker and Tamino.)*
Second Priest: What do I see? Friend, arise! What has befallen you?
Pap.: I am lying in a faint!
2nd Pr.: Arise! Collect yourself, and be a man!
Pap. *(rises)*: But tell me, Sir, why must I become acquainted with all these torments and horrors? If the gods really have selected a Papagena for me, why do I have to exert myself so hard to win her?
2nd Pr.: Let your reason answer that inquisitive question. Come, my duty demands that I lead you onwards. *(Covers Papageno's head with a veil.)*
Pap.: With such eternal wandering, one really feels like giving up love forever. *(Exeunt Second Priest and Papageno.)*

(Change of scene. Garden. Pamina asleep under the rosebushes.)
Monostatos: Ha, here I find the prudish beauty! What man could remain cold and unmoved before such a vision! The fire which burns within me will surely consume me. *(He looks around.)* If I knew—that I was all alone and unobserved—One little kiss, I should think, could be excused.

softly up to Pamina. The Queen appears suddenly, with thunder and lightning.)

Königin (*zu Monostatos*): Zurück!

Pamina (*erwacht*): Ihr Götter!

Monostatos (*prallt zurück*): O weh!—Die Göttin der Nacht.

Pam.: Mutter! Mutter! meine Mutter! (*Sie fällt ihr in die Arme.*)

Mon.: Mutter? Hm, das muss man von weitem belauschen. (*Schleicht ab.*)

Königin: Verdank es der Gewalt, mit der man dich mir entriss, dass ich noch deine Mutter mich nenne.—Siehst du hier diesen Stahl?—Er ist für Sarastro geschliffen.—Du wirst ihn töten. (*Sie dringt ihr den Dolch auf.*)

Pam.: Aber, liebste Mutter!—

Königin: Kein Wort!

Queen (*to Monostatos*): Away with you!

Pamina (*awakes*): O Gods!

Monostatos (*startled, jumps back*): What's this?—The Queen of the Night!

Pam.: Mother! Mother! My mother! (*Falls into her arms.*)

Mon. (*aside*): Mother? Hm! I'll have to watch this from a distance.

Queen: You may thank the power by which you were torn from me, that I still call myself your mother. Do you see this dagger? It has been sharpened for Sarastro. You will kill him—

Pam.: But dearest Mother—

Queen: Not a word!

mehr,
more,

mei - ne Toch - ter nim - mer-
I shall know you nev - er-

fp fp fp fp

mehr,
more,

so bist du mei - ne Toch - ter nim - mer-
Then as my child I know you nev - er-

fp fp fp cresc. f

mehr.
more.

p

al - le   Ban-de der Na - tur, wenn nicht   durch dich   Sa - ra-stro wird er-
all   the   force of na - ture's   tie   If not   through you   Sa - ra-stro's life be

blas - - - sen!   Hört!   hört!   hört!
tak - - en!   Hark!   Hark!   Hark!

_ Rache-götter!   Hört!   derMutterSchwur!   (Exit. Thunder.)
_ Gods of vengeance,   hear   a mother's cry!

Pam. (*den Dolch in der Hand*): Morden soll ich?—Götter, das kann ich nicht!—das kann ich nicht! (*Steht in Gedanken. Monostatos kommt schnell, heimlich und freudig.*) Götter, was soll ich tun?
Mon.: Dich mir anvertrauen. (*Nimmt ihr den Dolch.*)
Pam. (*erschrickt*): Ha!
Mon.: Warum zitterst du? Vor meiner schwarzen Farbe, oder vor dem ausgedachten Mord?
Pam. (*schüchtern*): Du weisst also?—
Mon.: Alles.—Du hast also nur einen Weg, dich und deine Mutter zu retten.
Pam.: Der wäre?
Mon.: Mich zu lieben.
Pam. (*zitternd, für sich*): Götter!
Mon.: Nun, Mädchen! Ja oder nein!
Pam. (*entschlossen*): Nein!
Mon. (*voll Zorn*): Nein? (*Sarastro tritt hinzu. Monostatos erhebt den Dolch.*) So fahre denn hin! (*Sarastro schleudert Monostatos zurück.*) Herr, ich bin unschuldig. (*Auf die Kniee fallend*)
Sar.: Ich weiss, dass deine Seele ebenso schwarz als dein Gesicht ist.—Geh!
Mon. (*im Abgehen*): Jetzt such ich die Mutter auf, weil die Tochter mir nicht beschieden ist. (*Ab.*)
Pam.: Herr, strafe meine Mutter nicht! Der Schmerz über meine Abwesenheit—
Sar.: Ich weiss alles. Du sollst sehen, wie ich mich an deiner Mutter räche.

Pam. (*dagger in hand*): I shall murder? Gods! I cannot, I cannot do that! (*Stands lost in thought. Monostatos comes to her side, quickly, stealthily, and with joy.*) What shall I do?
Mon.: Confide yourself in me. (*Takes the dagger away from her.*)
Pam. (*frightened*): Ah!
Mon.: Why do you tremble? Because I am black, or because of the murder that is planned?
Pam. (*timidly*): You know, then?
Mon.: Everything. There is only one way for you to save yourself and your mother.
Pam.: And that is?
Mon.: To love me!
Pam. (*trembling, aside*): O Gods!
Mon.: Well, maiden, yes or no?
Pam. (*firmly*): No!
Mon. (*angrily*): No? (*Enter Sarastro. Monostatos raises the dagger.*) Then die! (*Sarastro holds Monostatos back.*) Lord, I am innocent! (*Falls upon his knees.*)
Sar.: I know that your soul is just as black as your face. Go!
Mon. (*while leaving*): Now I shall look up the mother, because the daughter is not meant for me. (*Exit.*)
Pam.: Sire, do not punish my mother. The sorrow over having lost me—
Sar.: I know everything. But you shall see how I take revenge upon your mother.

No. 15. Aria

beß - re, beß - - re Land.
Mensch, ein Mensch zu sein. *(Exeunt.)*
bet - ter, bet - ter land.
gods', the gods' de - light.

(Verwandlung. Eine kurze Halle. Tamino und Papageno werden ohne Schleier von den zwei Priestern hereingeführt.)

Sprecher: Hier seid ihr euch beide allein überlassen.—Sobald die Posaune tönt, dann nehmt ihr euren Weg *(nach rechts zeigend)* dahin.—Prinz, lebt wohl! Noch einmal, vergesst das Wort nicht: Schweigen. *(Ab.)*

Zweiter Priester: Papageno, wer an diesem Ort sein Stillschweigen bricht, den strafen die Götter durch Donner und Blitz. Leb wohl! *(Ab. Tamino setzt sich auf eine Bank.)*

Pap. *(nach einer Pause)*: Tamino!

Tam.: St!

Pap.: Das ist ein lustiges Leben!—Wär ich lieber in meiner Strohhütte, oder im Wald, so hört ich doch manchmal einen Vogel pfeifen.

Tam. *(verweisend)*: St!

Pap.: Mit mir selbst werd ich wohl sprechen dürfen; und auch wir zwei können zusammen sprechen, wir sind ja Männer.

Tam. *(verweisend)*: St!

Pap. *(singt)*: La la la—la la la!—Nicht einmal einen Tropfen Wasser bekommt man bei diesen Leuten, viel weniger sonst was. *(Ein altes hässliches Weib kommt mit einem grossen Becher mit Wasser. Papageno sieht sie lange an.)* Ist das für mich?

Weib: Ja, mein Engel!

Pap. *(sieht sie wieder an, trinkt)*: Nicht mehr und nicht weniger als Wasser.—Sag du mir, du unbekannte Schöne, werden alle fremden Gäste auf diese Art bewirtet?

Weib: Freilich, mein Engel!

Pap.: So, so!—Auf diese Art werden die Fremden auch nicht gar zu häufig kommen.—

Weib: Sehr wenig.

Pap.: Kann mir's denken.—Geh, Alte, setze dich her zu mir, mir ist die Zeit verdammt lange.—*(Weib setzt sich zu ihm.)* Sag mir, wie alt bist du denn?

Weib: Wie alt?

Pap.: Ja!

Weib: Achtzehn Jahr und zwei Minuten.

Pap.: Achtzig Jahr und zwei Minuten?

Weib: Achtzehn Jahr und zwei Minuten.

Pap.: Ha ha ha!—Ei, du junger Engel! Hast du auch einen Geliebten?

Weib: I, freilich!

Pap.: Ist er auch so jung wie du?

Weib: Nicht ganz, er ist um zehn Jahre älter.—

Pap.: Um zehn Jahre ist er älter als du?—Das muss eine Liebe sein!—Wie nennt sich denn dein Liebhaber?

Weib: Papageno!

Pap. *(erschrickt, Pause)*: Papageno?—Wo ist er denn, dieser Papageno?

Weib: Da sitzt er, mein Engel!

Pap.: Ich wär dein Geliebter?

Weib: Ja, mein Engel!

Pap.: Sag mir, wie heisst du denn?

Weib: Ich heisse—*(Starker Donner, die Alte hinkt schnell ab.)*

Pap.: O weh! *(Tamino steht auf, droht mit dem Finger.)* Nun sprech ich kein Wort mehr! *(Die drei Knaben bringen Flöte und Glockenspiel.)*

(Change of scene. A short hallway. Tamino and Papageno, without the veils, are led in by the two Priests.)

Speaker: Once more you are both left by yourselves. As soon as you hear the trumpet call, start on your way in this direction. *(Points to the right.)* Prince, farewell. Once more, do not forget the word: silence. *(Exit.)*

Second Priest: Papageno, anyone who breaks his silence in this place is punished by the gods with thunder and lightning. Farewell. *(Exit. Tamino sits on a bench.)*

Pap. *(after a pause)*: Tamino!

Tam.: Sh!

Pap.: This is a jolly life! If only I were in my straw hut or in the woods, at least I would hear a bird sing once in a while.

Tam. *(reprimanding)*: Sh!

Pap.: Well, I should think at least I am allowed to talk to myself! And also, we two can talk to each other, because we are men.

Tam. *(reprimanding)*: Sh!

Pap. *(sings)*: La la la—la la la. Not even a single drop of water does one get from these people, let alone anything else. *(An old, ugly Woman appears, a big cup in her hands. Papageno looks at her for a long time.)* Is that for me?

Woman: Yes, my angel!

Pap. *(looks at her again, drinks)*: No more, no less than water. Tell me, you unknown beauty, are all foreign guests treated in this same fashion?

Wom.: Surely, my angel.

Pap.: Is that so? In that case, the foreigners don't come too frequently, I guess.

Wom.: Very seldom.

Pap.: That's what I thought. Come, Grandma, sit down here with me. I feel frightfully bored here. *(The Woman sits down at his side.)* You tell me, how old are you?

Wom.: How old?

Pap.: Yes.

Wom.: Eighteen years and two minutes.

Pap.: Eighty years and two minutes?

Wom.: Eighteen years and two minutes.

Pap.: Ha ha ha! Well, you young angel! Tell me, do you have a sweetheart?

Wom.: Naturally.

Pap.: And is he as young as you are?

Wom.: Not quite, he is ten years older.

Pap.: Ten years older than you are? That must be quite a fiery love! What is the name of your sweetheart?

Wom.: Papageno.

Pap. *(falls from his seat)*: Papageno? Where is he then, this Papageno?

Wom.: He is sitting right here, my angel.

Pap.: [Extempore: There he was sitting.] So I am your sweetheart?

Wom.: Yes, my angel.

Pap.: Tell me, what is your name?

Wom.: My name is—*(Loud thunder. Woman quickly hobbles away.)*

Pap.: Oh, oh! *(Tamino rises, shakes a warning finger at him.)* From now on I won't speak another word! *(The Three Spirits bring flute and bells.)*

No. 16. Trio

froh davon. / all amend. | Wenn wir zum drit-ten-mal uns se - hen, / When for the third time aid we prof-fer | ist Freude eu - res Mu-tes Lohn. / Hardship and trou-ble are at end.

froh davon. / all amend. | Wenn wir zum drit-ten-mal uns se - hen, / When for the third time aid we prof-fer, | ist Freude eu - res Mu-tes Lohn / Hardship and trou-ble are at end

Ta-mi-no Mut! / Ta-mi-no, hear: | nah ist das Ziel. / triumph you will.

Ta-mi-no Mut! / Ta-mi-no, hear: | nah ist das Ziel. / triumph you will.

Du Pa-pageno, / You, Pa-pa-ge-no, | schweige still, / pray be still.

Du Pa-pageno, / You, Pa-pa-ge-no, | schweige still, / pray be still,

still, still, schwei-ge still, still, still, schwei-ge still!
still, still, pray be still, still, still. pray be still!

still, still, schwei-ge still, still, still, schwei-ge still!
still, still, pray be still, still, still, pray be still!

(During the Trio they hand Tamino the flute and Papageno the glocken-spiel; then they withdraw.)

Pap.: Tamino, wollen wir nicht speisen? (*Tamino bläst auf seiner Flöte. Papageno isst.*) Blase du nur fort auf deiner Flöte, ich will meine Brocken blasen.—Herr Sarastro führt eine gute Küche.—Auf die Art, ja, da will ich schon schweigen, wenn ich immer solche gute Bissen bekomme.—Nun, ich will sehen, ob auch der Keller so gut bestellt ist. (*Er trinkt.*) Ha! das ist Götterwein! (*Die Flöte schweigt.*)

Pamina (*freudig eintretend*): Du hier?—Gütige Götter! Dank euch! Ich hörte deine Flöte—und so lief ich pfeilschnell dem Tone nach.—Aber du bist traurig?—Sprichst nicht eine Silbe mit deiner Pamina? Liebst du mich nicht mehr? (*Tamino seufzt und winkt ihr fort.*) Papageno, sage du mir, sag, was ist meinem Freund? (*Papageno hat einen Brocken in dem Munde, winkt ihr fortzugehen.*) Wie? Auch du? O, das ist mehr als Tod! (*Pause.*) Liebster, einziger Tamino!

Pap.: Tamino, shall we not have something to eat? (*Tamino plays on his flute. Papageno eats.*) You just keep on playing your flute, and I will play a game for myself! Mr. Sarastro certainly has a good cook. This way I would not mind keeping quiet, if I am always treated to such good food. Now I will see if his cellar is as good as his kitchen. (*Drinks.*) Ha, this is wine fit for the gods! (*The flute is silent.*)

Pamina (*entering joyfully*): You here? Kindly Gods! I thank you. I heard the sound of your flute and I followed the tone swift as an arrow. But you are sad? You speak no word to your Pamina? (*Tamino sighs and motions her away.*) Do you love me no more? (*Tamino sighs again.*) Papageno, you tell me what troubles my friend? (*Papageno has his mouth full, amd motions her away.* Hm, hm, hm!) You, too? Oh, this is worse than death! (*Pause.*) My dearest Tamino!

No. 17. Aria

Andante

Ach, ich fühl's, es ist verschwunden, e-wig hin mein gan-zes Glück, e-wig
Ah, I feel, to grief and sad-ness, Ev-er turned is love's de-light, Ev-er

sein, fühlst du nicht der Lie-be Sehnen, fühlst du nicht der Lie-be Sehnen, so___ wird
lone. If for love you do not languish, If for love you do not languish, Peace___ I

Ru-he, so___ wird Ruh im To-de sein, so wird Ruh___ im To___-de sein, im To-de
find___ then, peace___ I find in death a-lone, peace I find___ in death___ a-lone, in death a-

sein, im To___-de sein. *(Exit slowly.)*
lone, in death___ a-lone.

Pap. (*isst hastig*): Nicht wahr, Tamino, ich kann auch schweigen, wenn's sein muss.—(*Er trinkt.*) Der Herr Koch und der Herr Kellermeister sollen leben! (*Dreimaliger Posaunenton. Tamino winkt Papageno, dass er mit ihm gehen soll.*) Geh du nur voraus, ich komm schon nach. (*Tamino will ihn mit Gewalt fortführen.*) Der Stärkere bleibt da! (*Tamino geht ab.*) Jetzt will ich mir's erst recht wohl sein lassen. Ich ging jetzt nicht fort, und wenn Herr Sarastro seine sechs Löwen an mich spannte. (*Die Löwen erscheinen.*) O Barmherzigkeit, ihr gütigen Götter! Tamino rette mich! Die Herren Löwen machen eine Mahlzeit aus mir. (*Tamino kommt zurück, bläst seine Flöte, die Löwen verschwinden.*) Ich gehe schon! Heiss du mich einen Schelmen, wenn ich dir nicht in allem folge. (*Dreimaliger Posaunenton.*) Das geht uns an.—Wir kommen schon.—Aber hör einmal, Tamino, was wird denn noch alles mit uns werden? (*Tamino deutet gen Himmel.*) Die Götter soll ich fragen? (*Tamino deutet Ja.*) Ja, die könnten uns freilich mehr sagen, als wir wissen! (*Dreimaliger Posaunenton. Tamino reisst ihn mit Gewalt fort.*) Eile nur nicht so, wir kommen noch immer zeitig genug, um uns braten zu lassen. (*Beide ab. Verwandlung. Das Innere einer Pyramide.*)

Pap. (*eats eagerly*): Isn't it true, Tamino, that I, too, can keep silent if need be? (*Drinks.*) Long live the chef and the wine steward! (*Three blasts of the trumpet. Tamino motions Papageno to go with him.*) You just go ahead, I'll come right after you. (*Tamino tries to lead him away by force.*) The strongest one stays here. (*Exit Tamino.*) Now I'll begin to have a good time. I would not leave now, even if Mr. Sarastro sent his six lions after me. (*The Lions appear.*) Have mercy! Ye good Gods! Tamino, save me! These lions will make a meal of me! (*Tamino returns, blows his flute, and the lions retire.*) I'm coming, I'm coming. Call me a rascal if I don't do everything you tell me. (*Three blasts of the trumpet.*) That is for us. We are coming! But hear, Tamino, whatever will become of us? (*Tamino points skyward.*) I should ask the gods? (*Tamino nods.*) Yes, they really could tell us more than we know. (*Three trumpet blasts. Tamino drags Papageno away by force.*) Don't hurry so much, we shall be there in time to be roasted! (*Exeunt both. Change of scene. The interior of a pyramid.*)

No. 18. Chorus of the Priests

(The Priests enter, led by Sarastro.)

sein Geist ist kühn, sein Herz ist rein, bald, bald, bald wird er
His heart is bold, and pure his mind: Soon, soon, soon will the

un - ser wür - dig — sein, bald, bald, bald wird er un - ser
gods be sat - is - fied. Soon, soon, soon will the gods be

wür - dig — sein, wür - dig — sein, wür - dig — sein.
sat - is - fied, sat - is - fied, sat - is - fied.

(Tamino wird hereingeführt.)

Sar.: Prinz, dein Betragen war bis hieher männlich und gelassen; nun hast du noch zwei gefährliche Wege zu wandern. Schlägt dein Herz noch ebenso warm für Pamina, und wünschest du einst als ein weiser Fürst zu regieren, so mögen die Götter dich ferner begleiten.— Deine Hand.—Man bringe Pamina! (Zwei Priester bringen Pamina, welche mit einem Schleier bedeckt ist.)

Pam.: Wo bin ich?—Saget, wo ist mein Jüngling?

Sar.: Er wartet deiner, um dir das letzte Lebewohl zu sagen.

Pam.: Das letzte Lebewohl?—

Sar.: Hier!

Pam. (entrückt): Tamino!

Tamino (sie von sich weisend): Zurück!

(Tamino is led in.)

Sar.: Prince, thus far your actions have been manly and patient. Now you have still two dangerous trials to undertake. If your heart still beats as warmly for Pamina, and if in time to come you wish to rule as a wise monarch, then may the gods lead you further. Your hand. Have Pamina brought here. (Two Priests bring her in, veiled.)

Pam.: Where am I? Where is Tamino?

Sar.: He awaits you, to bid you a last farewell.

Pam.: A last farewell?

Sar.: Here.

Pam. (joyfully): Tamino!

Tamino (motions her to stay away): Away!

No. 19. Trio

keh - - - - re wie - - der. Le - be
end _____ this griev - - ing. Fare _ you

keh - - - - re wie - - der. Le - be
end _____ this griev - - ing. Fare _ you

wir sehn uns wie - der,
but not for- ev - er,

wohl! Le - be wohl!
well! Fare you well!

wohl! Le - be wohl! (*Pamina is led away by two Priests. Sarastro*
well! Fare_ you well! *withdraws with Tamino; the Priests follow.*)

wir sehn uns wie - der.
but not for- ev - er!

m. d.

(*Es wird dunkel.*)

Pap. (*von aussen*): Tamino! Tamino! Willst du mich denn gänzlich verlassen? (*kommt tappend herein.*) Wenn ich nur wenigstens wüsste, wo ich wäre.—Tamino!—Tamino!—So lang ich lebe, bleib ich nicht mehr von dir!—Nur diesmal verlass mich armen Reisegefährten nicht! (*Er kommt an die Tür links vorn.*)

Eine Stimme (*ruft*): Zurück! (*Donnerschlag; das Feuer schlägt zur Tür heraus.*)

Pap.: Barmherzige Götter!—Wo wend ich mich hin? Wenn ich nur wüsste, wo ich hereinkam! (*Er kommt an die Türe, wo er hereinkam.*)

Die Stimme: Zurück! (*Donner und Feuer wie oben.*)

Pap.: Nun kann ich weder vorwärts noch zurück! (*Weint.*) Muss vielleicht am Ende gar verhungern!—Schon recht!—Warum bin ich mitgereist.

Sprecher (*mit einer Fackel*): Mensch! Du hättest verdient, auf immer in finsteren Klüften der Erde zu wandern—die gütigen Götter aber entlassen dich der Strafe.—Dafür aber wirst du das himmlische Vergnügen der Eingeweihten nie fühlen.

Pap.: Je nun, es gibt noch mehr Leute meinesgleichen!—Mir wäre jetzt ein gutes Glas Wein das grösste Vergnügen.

Sprecher: Sonst hast du keinen Wunsch in dieser Welt?

Pap.: Bis jetzt nicht.

Sprecher: Man wird dich damit bedienen!—(*Ab. Sogleich kommt ein grosser Becher, mit rotem Wein angefüllt, aus der Erde.*)

Pap.: Juchhe! da ist er schon!—(*Trinkt.*) Herrlich!—Himmlisch!—Göttlich!—Ha! ich bin jetzt so vergnügt, dass ich bis zur Sonne fliegen wollte, wenn ich Flügel hätte!—Ha!—Mir wird ganz wunderlich ums Herz!—Ich möchte—ich wünschte—ja, was denn?

(*It becomes dark.*)

Pap. (*offstage*): Tamino! Tamino! Are you leaving me all alone? (*Enters, feeling his way.*) If I only knew where I was! Tamino! Tamino! As long as I live I shall never leave your side again. Just this once don't desert your poor fellow traveller! (*He comes to the door through which Tamino has left.*)

A Voice (*from outside*): Halt! (*Thunder; flames burst from the door.*)

Pap.: Merciful Gods, where shall I turn? If I only knew where I came in! (*Comes to the door where he had entered.*)

Voice (*from outside*): Halt! (*Thunder: flames burst from the door.*)

Pap.: Now I can go neither forwards nor backwards. (*Cries.*) Perhaps I will have to starve here! Serves me right! Why did I come with him?

Speaker (*with a torch*): Miserable! You deserve to wander forever in the dark abysses of the earth! But the clement gods exempt you from this punishment. However, you shall never experience the heavenly pleasures of the ordained.

Pap.: I don't care a fig about the ordained. Anyway, there are more people like me in the world. At the moment, to me the greatest pleasure would be a glass of wine.

Speaker: Other than this you have no further wish in the world?

Pap.: Not so far.

Speaker: You shall be served with it. (*Exit. A big cup filled with wine appears at once.*)

Pap.: Hurrah! There it is already! (*Drinks.*) Marvellous! Heavenly! Divine! Ha! I am so delighted now that I should like to fly to the sun, if I had wings. Ha! Something queer is happening in my heart! I want—I wish—but what?

No. 20. Aria

Andante

Papageno *(plays the glockenspiel)*

1. Ein Mädchen o - der Weib - chen wünscht Pa - pa - ge - no
1. I'd give my fin - est feath - er To find a pret - ty

sich, o, so ein sanf - tes Täub - chen wär Se - lig - keit für
wife. Two tur - tle-doves to - geth - er, We'd share a hap - py

mich, wär Se - lig-keit für mich, wär Se - lig-keit für mich.
life! We'd share a hap-py life! We'd share a hap-py life!

Allegro

Dann schmeckte mir Trinken und
And hap - pi - ly then ev - er

Papageno

2. Ein Mädchen o - der Weib - chen wünscht Pa - pa - ge - no
2. I'd give my fin - est feath - er To find a pret - ty

sich, o, so ein sanf - tes Täub - chen wär Se - lig - keit für
wife. Two tur - tle - doves to - geth - er, We'd share a hap - py

mich, wär Se - lig-keit für mich. wär Se - lig-keit für mich.
life! We'd share a hap-py life! We'd share a hap-py life!

Allegro

Ach kann ich denn keiner von a-
I'm sure there are girls all a-

al - len den rei - zenden Mädchen ge - fal - len? helf ei - ne mir nur aus der Not, sonst
round me, But none of them seems to have found me. With no one to love me or care, I'll

cresc.

fp

gram ich mich wahrlich zu Tod,   Ach! kann ich   denn keiner   ge-
cer-tain-ly die of de-spair.   With   no one   to   love me   or

fal-len? helf ei-ne mir nur aus der Not,— sonst gräm ich mich wahrlich zu Tod.
care,— with no one to love me or care,— I'll cer-tain-ly die of de-spair!

cresc.   *fp*

mich wahrlich zu Tod,   mich wahrlich zu Tod,
I'll die of de-spair,   I'll die of de-spair!

Andante

Papageno

3. Ein
3. I'd

Mund, so bin ich schon wieder ge-sund,— so bin ich schon wieder ge-sund,
kiss— To put me in heav-en-ly bliss,— To put me in heav-en-ly bliss,

schon wieder ge-sund, schon wieder ge-sund.
in heav-en-ly bliss, in heav-en-ly bliss.

(Das alte Weib, tanzend, und auf ihren Stock dabei sich stützend, kommt herein.)

Weib: Da bin ich schon, mein Engel!

Pap.: Du hast dich meiner erbarmt?

Weib: Ja, mein Engel!

Pap.: Das ist ein Glück!

Weib: Und wenn du mir versprichst, mir ewig treu zu bleiben, dann sollst du sehen, wie zärtlich dein Weibchen dich lieben wird.

Pap.: Ei, du zärtliches Närrchen!

Weib: O, wie will ich dich umarmen, dich liebkosen, dich an mein Herz drücken!

Pap.: Auch ans Herz drücken?

Weib: Komm, reich mir zum Pfand unseres Bundes deine Hand!

Pap.: Nur nicht so hastig, lieber Engel! So ein Bündnis braucht doch auch seine Überlegung.

Weib: Papageno, ich rate dir, zaudre nicht!—Deine Hand, oder du bist auf immer hier eingekerkert.

Pap.: Eingekerkert?

Weib: Wasser und Brot wird deine tägliche Kost sein.— Ohne Freund, ohne Freundin musst du leben, und der Welt auf immer entsagen.

Pap.: Wasser trinken?—der Welt entsagen?—Nein, da will ich doch lieber eine Alte nehmen, als gar keine.— Nun, da hast du meine Hand mit der Versicherung, dass ich dir immer getreu bleibe, *(für sich)* so lang' ich keine Schönere sehe.

Weib: Das schwörst du?

Pap.: Ja, das schwör ich! *(Weib verwandelt sich in ein junges Mädchen, welches ebenso gekleidet ist, wie Papageno.)* Pa-Pa-Papagena!—*(Er will sie umarmen.)*

Sprecher *(kommt und nimmt sie bei der Hand):* Fort mit dir, junges Weib! Er ist deiner noch nicht würdig! *(Er drängt sie hinaus, Papageno will nach.)* Zurück! sag ich.

Pap.: Eh ich mich zurückziehe, soll die Erde mich verschlingen. *(Er sinkt hinab.)* O ihr Götter! *(Er springt wieder heraus und läuft ab. Verwandlung. Kurzer Palmengarten.)*

(The old Woman enters, hobbling and supporting herself on her stick.)

Woman: Here I am, my angel!

Pap.: So you took pity on me, then?

Wom.: Yes, my angel.

Pap.: What wonderful luck I have!

Wom.: And if you promise to be true to me forever, then you will see how tenderly your little wife will love you.

Pap.: Oh, what a tender goose you are!

Wom.: Oh, how I shall embrace you, caress you, press you to my heart!

Pap.: Even press me to your heart?

Wom.: Come, give me your hand as a pledge of our union.

Pap.: Not so fast, dear angel! Such a marriage needs some consideration, after all.

Wom.: Papageno, I advise you, don't hesitate! Your hand, or you shall be imprisoned here forever.

Pap.: Imprisoned?

Wom.: Bread and water shall be your daily diet. You must live without friends or sweetheart and renounce the world forever.

Pap.: Renounce the world forever? Drink water? No! In that case I'll take an old one rather than none at all. Well, here you have my hand with the assurance that I shall always be true to you *(aside)* until I find someone prettier.

Wom.: You swear that?

Pap.: Yes, I swear it. *(Woman changes into a maiden, dressed like Papageno.)* Pa-Pa-Papagena! *(He wishes to embrace her.)*

Speaker *(enters and takes her by the hand):* Begone, young woman! He is not yet worthy of you. *(He drags her out. Papageno wants to follow.)* Back, I say, or woe unto you!

Pap.: Before I withdraw, the earth shall swallow me up! *(He sinks into the earth.)* Oh, Gods above! *(Jumps out of the trap. Extempore: Sir, how dare you meddle in my family affairs? Change of scene. Palm garden.)*

No. 21. Finale

Andante

sotto voce

* f* *p*

1st & 2nd Spirits

Bald prangt, den Morgen zu ver - kün - den, die
Soon speeds the morning light pro - claim - ing   The

3rd Spirit

Bald prangt, den Morgen zu ver - kün - den, die
Soon speeds the morning light pro - claim - ing   The

f *p*
f

Sonn auf gold-ner   Bahn, bald soll der A-ber-glaube schwinden, bald   siegt der wei - se
sunshines gold-en   way.— This youth, the pow'rs of dark de - fam-ing, Shall   see   the light of

Sonn auf gold-ner   Bahn, bald soll der A-ber-glaube schwinden, bald. siegt der wei - se
sun- shine's gold-en   way.— This youth, the pow'rs of dark de - fam-ing, Shall   see   the light   of

Mann.   O   hol - de Ruhe, steig her - nieder, kehr in der Menschen Herzen wieder,   dann
day.—   O   calmness from a-bove de - scending,   Reprieve all   men from grief un - end-ing.   Then

Mann.   O   hol - de Ruhe, steig her - nieder, kehr in der Men-schen Herzen wie-der,   dann
day.—   O   calmness from a-bove de - scending,   Reprieve all men   from grief un - end-ing.   Then

(pointing to the dagger)

Mann, den ich nimmermehr kann hassen, sei-ne Traute kann ver-las-sen. Dies gab mei-ne Mut-ter
vow That despairing I have tak-en; By my love I am for-sak-en! This my moth-er gave to

cresc. *fp*

mir.   **Pamina**
me! **1st & 2nd Spirits**   Lieber durch dies Ei-sen sterben, als durch Lie-
                             Rath-er by this blade I per-ish, Than a love-

Selbst-mord strafet Gott an dir!
3rd Spirit Heav-en's law will chasten thee!

Selbst-mord strafet Gott an dir!
Heav-en's law will chasten thee!

fp

- besgram ver-derben, Mutter, Mutter! durch dich lei-de ich und dein Fluch verfolget mich.
less life to cherish. Mother, Mother! Your curse is my bane And through you I suf-fer pain.

p   *fp*

Pamina

1st & 2nd Spirits   Ha! des Jam-mers Maß ist voll!   fal-scher
                        No! I drain the cup of woe!   Faith-less

Mädchen, willst du mit uns gehn?
Maid-en, will you come with us?

3rd Spirit
Mädchen, willst du mit uns gehn?
Maid-en, will you come with us?

die Göt - ter schüt - zen sie, schüt - zen sie, schüt - zen sie. *(exit.)*
will keep them — safe from harm, safe — from harm, safe — from harm.

Göt - ter selb - sten schüt - zen sie, schüt - zen sie, schüt - zen sie. *(exeunt.)*
gods will keep them — safe — from — harm, safe — from harm, safe — from harm.

Göt - ter selb - sten schüt - zen sie, schüt - zen sie, schüt - zen sie. *(exit.)*
gods will keep them safe from harm, safe from harm, safe from harm.

(Change of scene. Rocky caves. At left, glowing fire; at right, a waterfall. Twilight.)

Adagio.

leuch - tet wird er dann im Stan - de sein,
light - ened, *he will now him - self pre - pare,*

sich den My - ste - ri - en der I - sis ganz zu
The ho - ly mys - ter - ies of I - sis all to

(Tamino is led in by the Two Priests.)

Tamino

weihn.
share.

Mich schreckt kein Tod als Mann zu
By fear of death I am not

handeln, den Weg der Tu - gend fort - zu - wandeln, schließt mir des Schrek - kens Pfor - ten
shak - en. The path of vir - tue I have tak - en. Un - lock the fa - tal doors to

Pamina *(offstage)*

auf; ich wage froh den küh - nen Lauf. Tami - no halt! ich muß dich
me; My course will firm and gal - lant be. Ta - mi - no, wait! I go with

Pamina *(embracing Tamino)*

Tamino

Ta - mi - no___ mein! O welch ein Glück! Pa - mi - na___ mein! o welch ein
Ta - mi - no___ mine! Oh, hap - py fate! Pa - mi - na___ mine! Oh, hap - py

Glück! *(points towards the rocky caves)*
fate!

Hier sind die Schreckens-
Be - yond those gates un-

pfor - ten, die Not und Tod mir dräun. Ich wer - de al - ler Or - ten an
fold - ing Both death and men - ace hide. Your ev - 'ry act up - hold - ing, I

Pamina

dei - ner Sei - te sein. Ich sel - ber füh - re dich. die
shall not leave your side.___ In me your trust con - fide, For

(She takes him by the hand.)

Lie - be lei - te mich. Sie mag den Weg mit Ro - sen streun, weil Rosen stets bei Dornen
Love shall be my guide. Our path with ros - es it a - dorns, For ros - es always grow with

sein. Spiel du die Zau-ber- -flö-te an, sie schüt-ze uns auf_ uns-rer
thorns. Now take the mag-ic_ flute and play; Its gold-en tones pro tect our

Bahn. Es schnitt in ei - ner Zauber-stun - de mein Vater sie aus tiefstem
way. 'Twas shaped at mid - night's witching hour By my fa-ther, with his mag-ic

Grun-de der tau-sendjährgen Eiche aus bei Blitz und Donner, Sturm und Braus. Nun
pow - er, From branch of oak tree, strong and old, While storm and thunder wild - ly rolled. Now

Pamina

komm und spiel die Flö-te an; sie lei - te uns auf_ grau - ser Bahn. Wir wan-deln
take the mag - ic flute and play; Its tones will guide our_ fear - some way. We wan - der

Tamino

Wir
We

To - des düst - re Nacht, düst - re Nacht, düst - re Nacht.
through the vale ___ of night, vale ___ of night, vale ___ of night.

To - des düst - re Nacht, düst - re Nacht, düst - re Nacht.
through the vale ___ of night, vale ___ of night, vale of night.

To - des düst - re Nacht, düst - re Nacht, düst - re Nacht.
through the vale ___ of night, vale of night, vale of night.

To - des düst - re Nacht, düst - re Nacht, düst - re Nacht.
through the vale of night, vale of night, vale of night.

mfp   *p*   *mf*   *p*

(*Tamino and Pamina pass through the fiery cave, she with her hand on Tamino's shoulder, while he plays his flute.*)

March
Adagio

(Change of scene without Curtain. Temple, brightly illuminated)

Pamina

Ihr Göt-ter, welch ein Au-gen-blick ge - wäh-ret ist uns I - sis Glück.
O Gods, what ec - sta-sy di - vine! On us the smiles of I - sis shine!

Tamino

Ihr Göt-ter, welch ein Au-gen-blick ge - wäh-ret ist uns I - sis Glück.
O Gods, what ec - sta-sy di - vine! On us the smiles of I - sis shine!

Allegro

Sopran.

Tri - umph, Tri-umph, Tri-umph, du ed - les Paar! be-sie-get

Alt.

Chorus *(offstage)* Re - joice! Re-joice! The vic - to - ry is gained! The journey's

Tenor

Tri - umph, Tri-umph, Tri-umph, du ed - les Paar! be-sie-get

Bass

Re-joice! Re-joice! The vic - to - ry is gained! The journey's

Allegro

f   *p*

hast du die Ge-fahr! der I - sis Wei - he ist nun dein! Kommt, kommt,
Come, come!

end you have at-tained! On you the smiles of I - sis shine! Come,

hast du die Ge-fahr! der I - sis Wei - he ist nun dein!

end you have at-tained! On you the smiles of I - sis shine! Come,

Mäd-chen, denkt an mich, schö-ne Mäd-chen, denkt an mich! Will sich
maid-ens, think of me, Love-ly maid-ens, think of me! Will not

ei - ne um mich Ar - men, eh ich hän - ge, noch er - bar - men, wohl so laß ich's dies - mal
some-one show com-pas-sion Ere I hang in such a fash-ion? Well, this once I let it

(looks around)

sein. Ru-fet nur: ja o-der nein, ru-fet nur: ja o-der nein! Kei-ne
go. Just re-ply: say yes or no, Just re-ply: say yes or no. No one

hört mich, al-les stil-le, al-les, al-les stil-le! Al-so ist es eu-er
an-swers, all is qui-et, here I stand de-sert-ed! Then my end can't be a-

Wil-le? Pa-pa-ge-no, frisch hin-auf, en-de dei-nen Le-bens-lauf! Pa-pa-
vert-ed. Pa-pa-ge-no, go a-head. Tie the noose and you are dead! Pa-pa-

sei mein Her-zens-täub-chen, mein Herzens-täub-chen, mein Her-zens - täub-chen!
be thy heart's own dar-ling, thy heart's own dar-ling, thy heart's own dar-ling!

mein lie-bes Weibchen, mein Her-zens - täub-chen!
my lit-tle star-ling; my lit-tle star-ling!

cresc.

Wel - che Freude wird das sein,
What a joy for us is near

Wel - che Freude wird das sein,
What a joy for us is near

wenn die Göt-ter uns be-
When the gods, their bounty

wenn die Göt-ter uns be - den-ken, uns-rer Lie-be Kin-der schen-ken, uns-rer Lie-be Kin-der
When the gods, their bounty showing, And their grace on us be-stow-ing, And their grace on us be-

den-ken,
showing,

uns-rer Lie-be Kin-der schenken, uns-rer Lie-be Kin-der
And their grace on us be-stow-ing, And their grace on us be-

ritard.

schen-ken, so lie-be klei-ne Kin-der - lein, Kin-der-lein,
stow-ing, Will send us ti-ny chil-dren dear, chil-dren dear,

Kin-der - lein.
chil-dren dear,

schen-ken, so lie-be klei-ne Kin-der - lein Kin-der - lein.
stow-ing, Will send us ti-ny chil-dren dear, chil-dren dear,

Kin-der - lein,
chil-dren dear,

ritard.

Kin - der - lein, so lie - be klei - ne Kin - der - lein, so lie - be klei - ne Kin - der -
chil - dren dear, such love - ly, ti - ny chil - dren dear, such love - ly, ti - ny chil - dren

Kin - der - lein, so lie - be klei - ne Kin - der - lein, so lie - be klei - ne Kin - der -
chil - dren dear, such love - ly, ti - ny chil - dren dear, such love - ly, ti - ny chil - dren

a tempo

lein.   Dann _____ ei - ne klei - ne Pa - pa -
dear.   Then _____ we will have a Pa - pa -

a tempo

lein. Erst _____ ei - nen klei - nen Pa - pa - ge - no.
dear. First _____ we will have a Pa - pa - ge - no.

a tempo

ge - na.   Dann _____ wie - der ei - ne Pa - pa -
ge - na.   Then _____ comes an - oth - er Pa - pa -

Dann _____ wie - der ei - nen Pa - pa - ge - no,
Then _____ comes an - oth - er Pa - pa - ge - no,

ge - na,   Pa - pa - ge - na,   Pa - pa - ge - na, Pa - pa - ge - na, Pa - pa - ge - na!
ge - na,   Pa - pa - ge - na,   Pa - pa - ge - na, Pa - pa - ge - na, Pa - pa - ge - na!

Pa - pa - ge - no.   Pa - pa - ge - no,   Pa - pa - ge - no, Pa - pa - ge - no!
Pa - pa - ge - no.   Pa - pa - ge - no,   Pa - pa - ge - no, Pa - pa - ge - no!

cresc.

(Change of scene. Rocky landscape. Night.)

Più moderato

(Enter Monostatos, the Queen, and the Three Ladies, with burning torches.)

Monost. Nur stil-le, stil-le, stil-le, stil-le, bald drin-gen wir in Tem-pel
Now still-y, still-y, still-y, still-y, As we ap-proach the tem-ple

Queen & 1st Lady

Nur stil-le, stil-le, stil-le, stil-le! bald drin-gen wir in Tem-pel ein.
Now still-y, still-y, still-y, still-y, As we approach the tem-ple door.

2nd & 3rd L.

Nur stil-le, stil-le, stil-le, stil-le! bald drin-gen wir in Tem-pel ein.
Now still-y, still-y, still-y, still-y. As we approach the tem-ple door.

ein.   Doch
door.   My

Monost.

Für-stin, hal--te Wort, er-fül-le, dein Kind muß mei-ne Gat-tin
la--dy, keep your word, ful-fill it: Your child must wed the faith-ful

Queen

sein. Ich hal-te Wort; es ist mein Wil-le! Mein Kind soll dei-ne Gat-tin
Moor. I keep my word, I firm-ly wish it! My child shall wed the faith-ful

(Thunder and sound of water.)

nich - tet ist un - se - re Macht,
tin - guished, de - feat - ed our might,
wir al - - le ge -
We plunge to de -

nich - tet ist un - se - re Macht,
tin - guished, de - feat - ed our might,
wir al - - le ge -
We plunge to de -

nich - tet ist un - se - re Macht,
tin - guished, de - feat - ed our might,
wir al - - le ge -
We plunge to de -

stür - zet in e - wi - ge Nacht!
struc - tion and in - fi - nite night.

stür - zet in e - wi - ge Nacht!
struc - tion and in - fi - nite night.
(They sink into the earth.)

stür - zet in e - wi - ge Nacht!
struc - tion and in - fi - nite night.
(Change of scene without Curtain. Temple of the Sun.
Sarastro stands on an eminence. Before him stand
Tamino and Pamina.)

Sarast.
Die Strahlen der Son - ne ver-trei-ben die Nacht,
The sun's radiant glo - ry has vanquished the night,
zer-nich-ten der Heuch-ler er-
The pow-ers of dark-ness have

Maestoso

Recit.

e - wi - ger Kron.
ceiv-ing — as prize.
Es sieg - te die Stär - ke und krö - net zum Lohn die

e - wi - ger Kron.
ceiv-ing — as prize.
Thus cour - age has tri - umphed and vir - tue will rise. The

mit e - wi - ger Kron.
re - ceiv-ing as prize.
Es sieg - te die Stär - ke und krö - net zum Lohn die

Schön - heit und Weis - heit mit e - wi - ger Kron, mit e - -
lau - rels of wis - dom re - ceiv - ing as prize. re ceiv -

wi - ger Kron, mit e - - wi - ger Kron!
ing as prize, re - ceiv ing as prize.

End of the Opera